Grades
PreK-1

The Complete Book of
Starter Spanish

ROJO (RED)

EL TRINEO (SLED)

LA NIEVE (SNOW)

Thinking Kids®
Carson-Dellosa Publishing LLC
Greensboro, North Carolina

Thinking Kids®
Carson-Dellosa Publishing LLC
P.O. Box 35665
Greensboro, NC 27425 USA

Printed in the USA • All rights reserved.   ISBN 978-1-4838-2685-1
06-139201151

Table of Contents

Name_____

Introductions and Greetings

Say the Spanish introductions and greetings out loud.

¡Hola!		Hello!
¿Cómo te llamas?		What is your name?
Me llamo...		My name is...

Name_____

Introductions and Greetings

Say the Spanish introductions and greetings out loud.

¿Cómo estás?	How are you?

bien

mal

así, así

¡Adiós!

Good-bye!

Name_____

Polite Words

Say the Spanish introductions and greetings out loud.

¿Cuántos años tienes?		How old are you?
Tengo seis años.		I am six years old.
por favor		please
gracias		thank you

Name_____

Polite Words

Say the Spanish introductions and greetings out loud.

| amigo |  | friend |

| amiga |  | friend |

| sí | no | amigos |  | friends |

| ¡Hasta Luego! |   | See you later! |

Name_____

Red

The Spanish word for red is **rojo**.

Color the pictures **rojo**.

Name _____

Red

Draw something else that is **rojo**.

Now, trace the word **rojo**.

Name_____

Red

Circle the picture that is **rojo** in each row.

Name_____

Red

Color the balloon **rojo**.
Color the pictures to match the balloon.

Name_____

Red

Read the word. Trace the word. Then, write the word on your own.

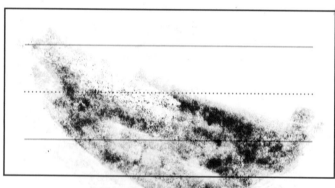 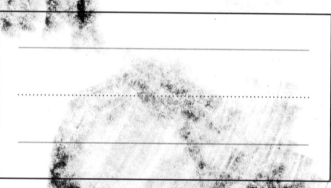

Color the word **rojo**.

Name_____

Red

Which three could be **rojo**?

Color with **rojo**.

rojo

Name_____

Color Review

Color the spaces marked **rojo** with the correct crayon.

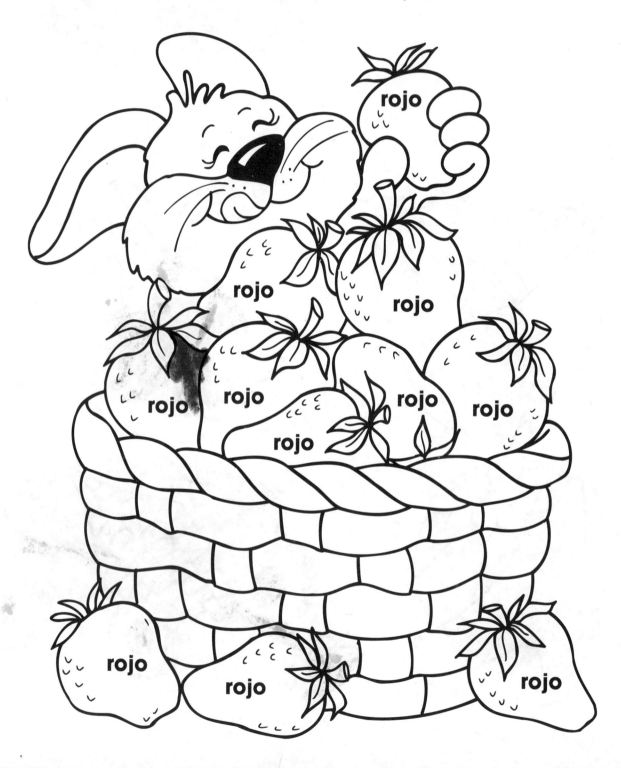

Name_____

Yellow

The Spanish word for yellow is amarillo.
Color the pictures amarillo.

Name_____

Yellow

Draw something else that is **amarillo**.

Now, trace the word **amarillo**.

Name_____

Yellow

Circle the picture that is **amarillo** in each row.

Name_____

Yellow

Color the balloon **amarillo**.

Color the pictures to match the balloon.

Name_____

Yellow

Read the word. Trace the word. Then, write the word on your own.

amarillo

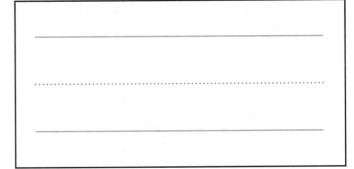

Color the word **amarillo**.

Name_____

Yellow

Which three could be **amarillo**?

Color with **amarillo**.

Name_____

Color Review

Color the spaces marked **rojo** and **amarillo** with the correct crayons.

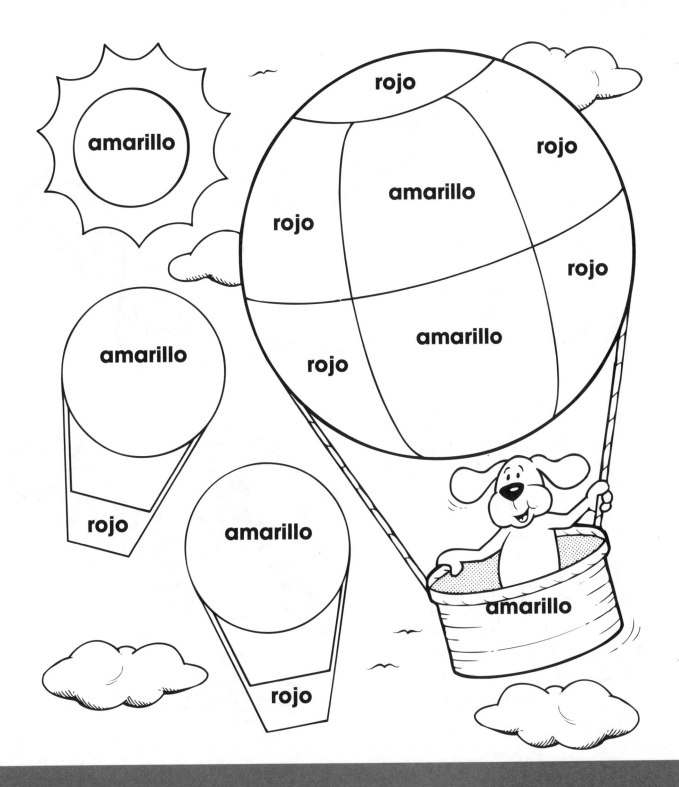

Name_____

Blue

The Spanish word for blue is **azul**.

Color the pictures **azul**.

Blue

Draw something else that is **azul**.

Now, trace the word **azul**.

Name_____

Blue

Circle the picture that is **azul** in each row.

Name_____

Blue

Color the balloon **azul**.

Color the pictures to match the balloon.

Name_____

Blue

Read the word. Trace the word. Then, write the word on your own.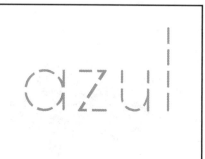

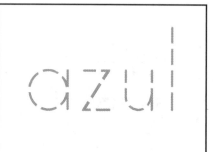

Color the word **azul**.

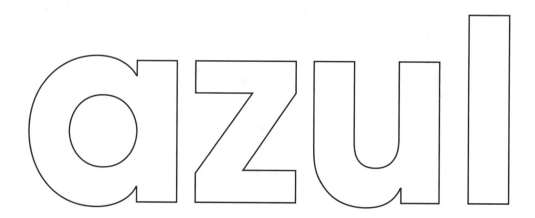

Name_____

Blue

Which three could be **azul**?

Color with **azul**.

Name_____

Color Review

Color the spaces marked **rojo**, **amarillo**, and **azul** with the correct crayons.

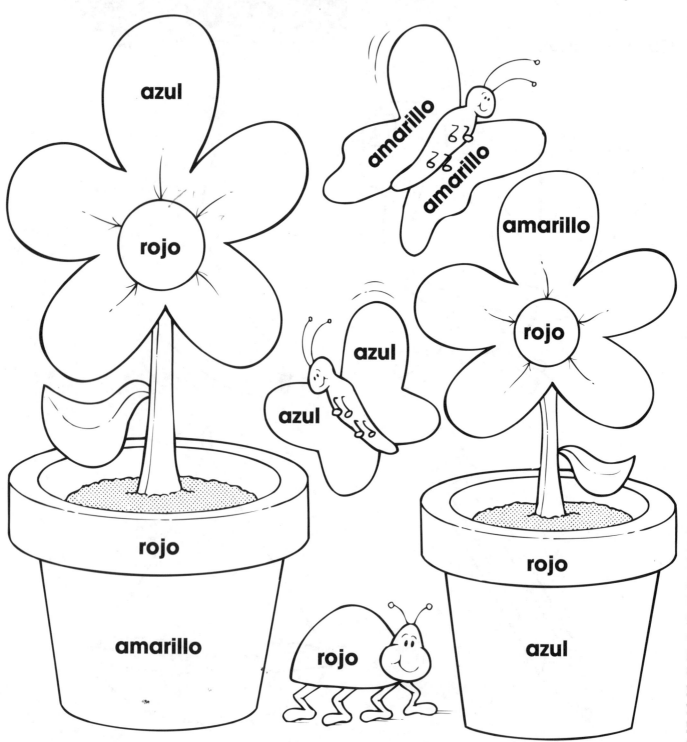

Name_____

Green

The Spanish word for green is **verde**.

Color the pictures **verde**.

Green

Draw something else that is **verde**.

Now, trace the word **verde**.

verde

Name_____

Green

Circle the picture that is **verde** in each row.

Name_____

Green

Color the balloon **verde**.
Color the pictures to match the balloon.

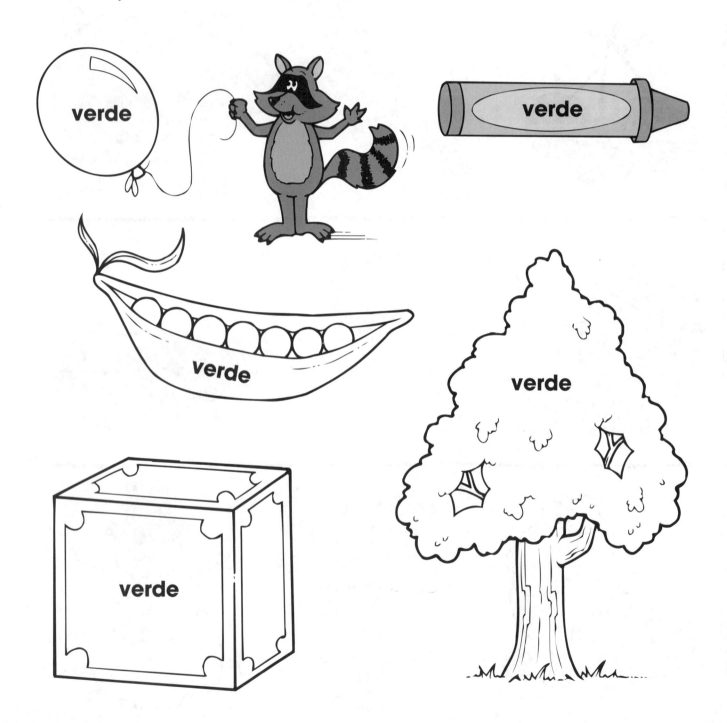

Green

Read the word. Trace the word. Then, write the word on your own. verde

| verde | verde | verde |

Color the word **verde**.

Name_____

Green

Which three could be **verde**?

Color with **verde**.

Name_____

Color Review

Color the spaces marked **rojo**, **amarillo**, **azul**, and **verde** with the correct crayons. Then, trace and color the petals.

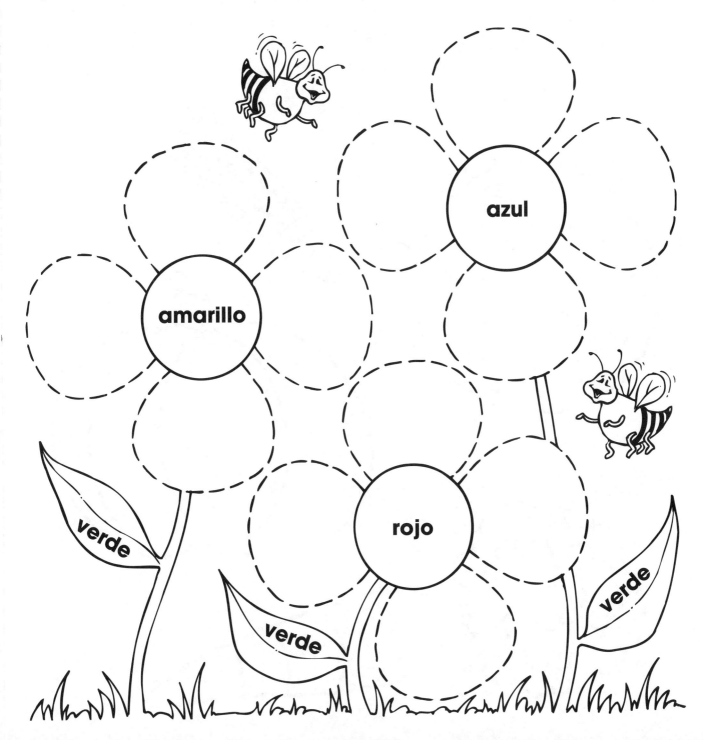

Name_____

Orange

The Spanish word for orange is naranja.
Color the pictures naranja.

Name_____

Orange

Draw something else that is **naranja**.

Now, trace the word **naranja**.

Name_____

Orange

Circle the picture that is **naranja** in each row.

Name_____

Orange

Color the balloon **naranja**.

Color the pictures to match the balloon.

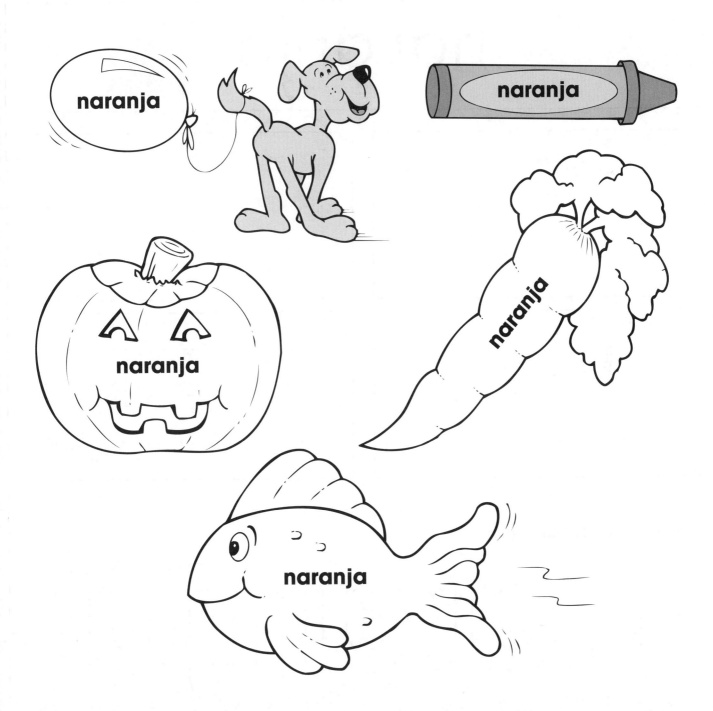

Name_____

Orange

Read the word. Trace the word. Then, write the word on your own.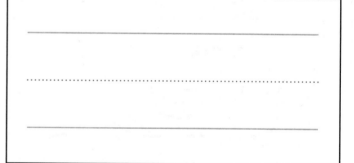

naranja

naranja

naranja

Color the word **naranja**.

Name_____

Orange

Which three could be **naranja**?

Color with **naranja**.

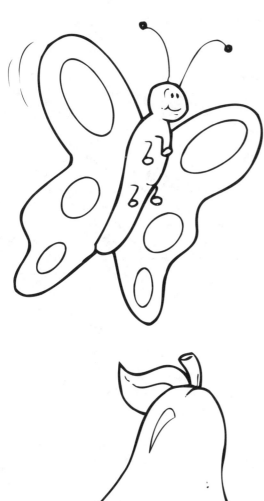

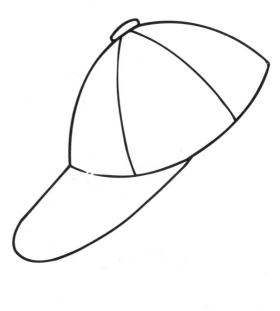

Name_____

Color Review

Color the spaces marked **rojo**, **amarillo**, **azul**, **verde**, and **naranja** with the correct crayons.

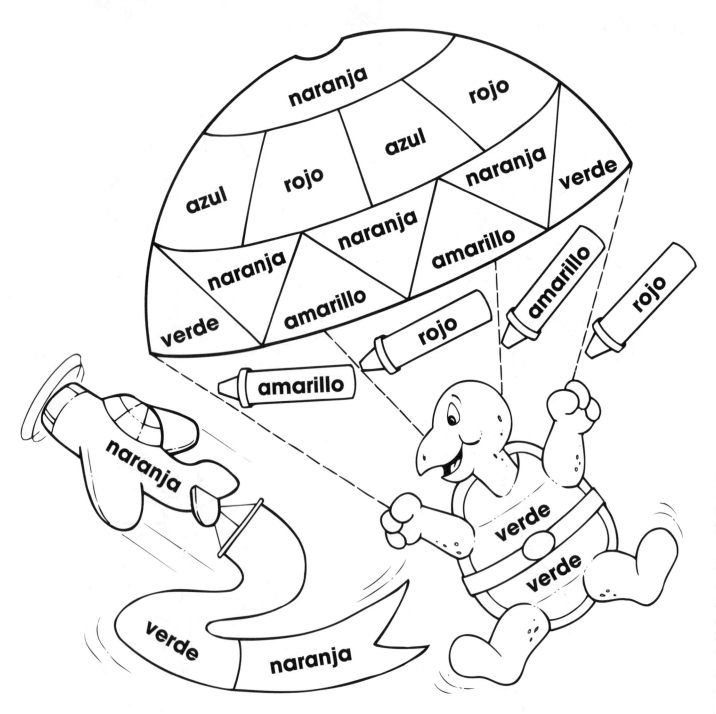

Name_____

Purple

The Spanish word for purple is **morado**.

Color the pictures **morado**.

Name_____

Purple

Draw something else that is **morado**.

Now, trace the word **morado**.

Name_____

Purple

Circle the picture that is **morado** in each row.

Name_____

Purple

Color the balloon **morado**.

Color the pictures to match the balloon.

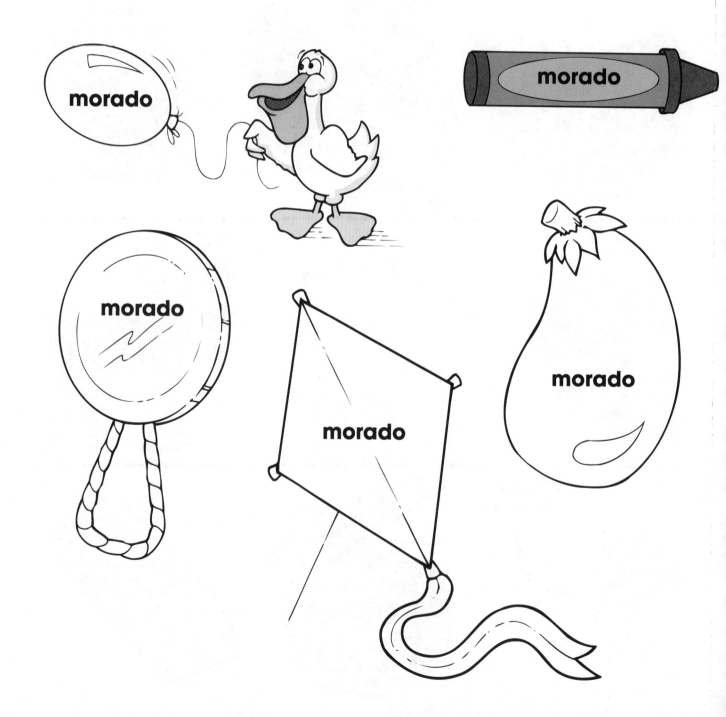

Name_____

Purple

Read the word. Trace the word. Then, write the word on your own.

morado

morado

morado

Color the word **morado**.

Name_____

Purple

Which three could be **morado**?

Color with **morado**.

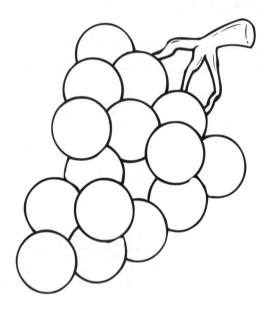

Name_____

Color Review

Color the spaces marked **rojo**, **amarillo**, **azul**, **verde**, **naranja**, and **morado** with the correct crayons.

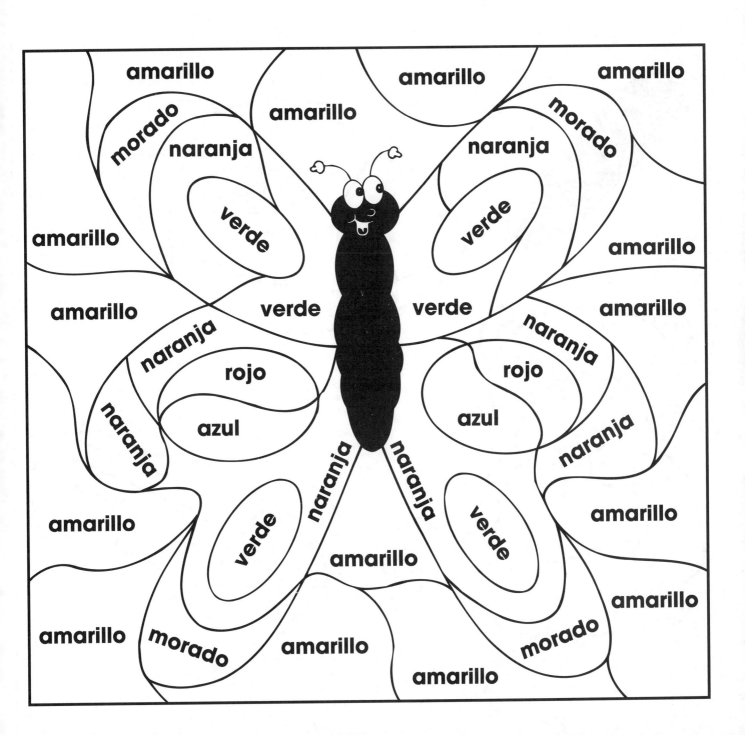

Name_____

Brown

The Spanish word for brown is **marrón**.
Color the pictures **marrón**.

Name_____

Brown

Draw something else that is **marrón**.

Now, trace the word **marrón**.

Name_____

Brown

Circle the picture that is **marrón** in each row.

Name_____

Brown

Color the hat **marrón**.

Color the pictures to match the hat.

Name_____

Brown

Read the word. Trace the word. Then, write the word on your own.

marrón

marrón

marrón

Color the word **marrón**.

Name_____

Brown

Which three could be **marrón**?

Color with **marrón**.

Name_____

Color Review

Color the spaces marked **rojo**, **amarillo**, **azul**, **verde**, **naranja**, **morado**, and **marrón** with the correct crayons.

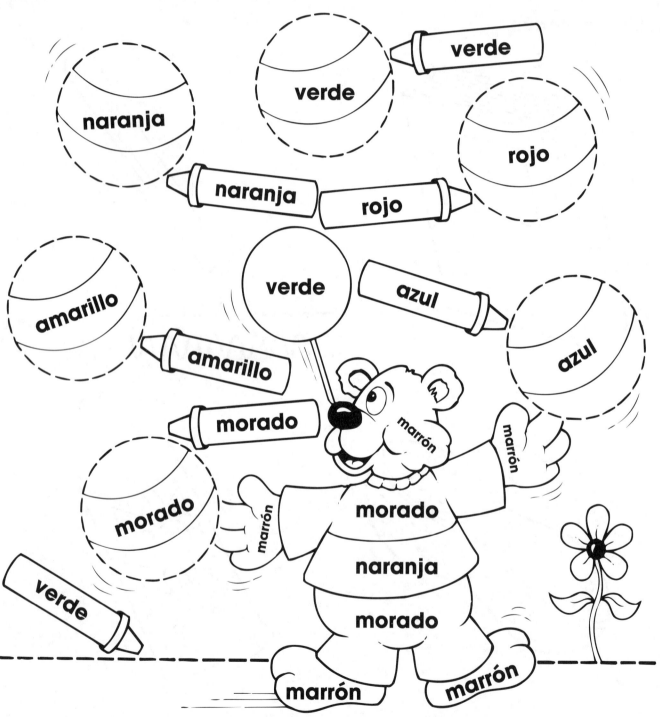

Name_____

Black

The Spanish word for black is **negro**.

Color the pictures **negro**.

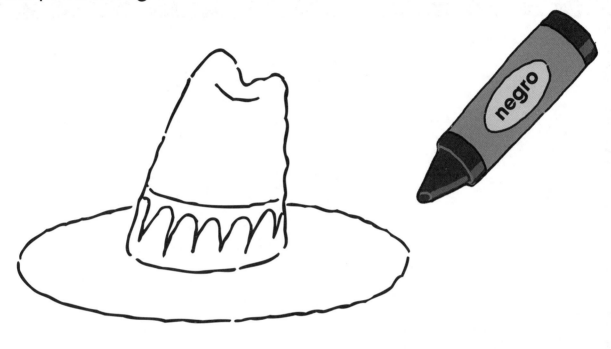

Name_____

Black

Draw something else that is **negro**.

Now, trace the word **negro**.

Name_____

Black

Circle the picture that is **negro** in each row.

Name_____

Black

Color the hat **negro**.
Color the pictures to match the hat.

Name_____

Black

Read the word. Trace the word. Then, write the word on your own.

negro

negro   negro

_____

_____

Color the word **negro**.

Name_____

Black

Which three could be **negro**?

Color with **negro**.

Name_____

Color Review

Color the pictures marked **rojo**, **amarillo**, **azul**, **verde**, **naranja**, **morado**, **marrón**, and **negro** with the correct crayons.

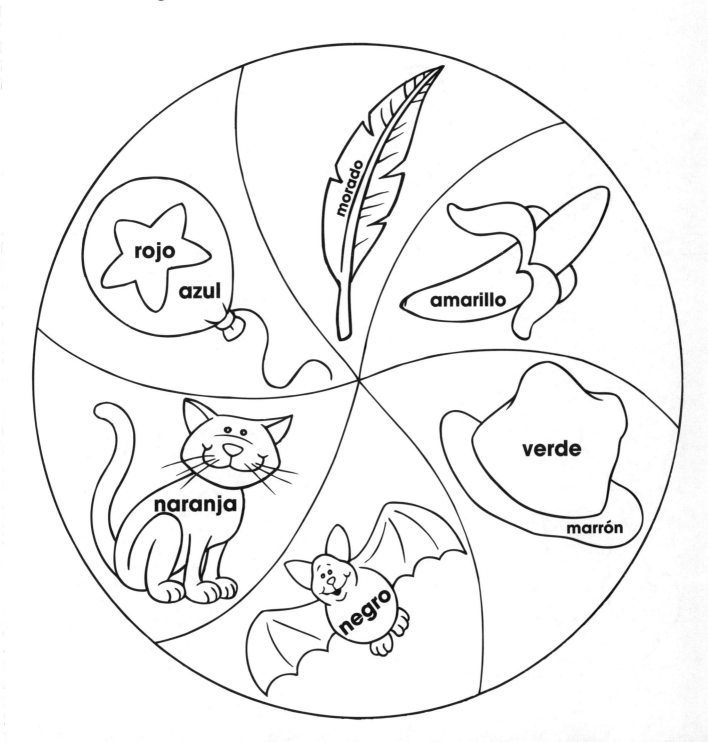

Name_____

White

The Spanish word for white is **blanco**.
Color the pictures **blanco**.

Name_____

White

Draw something else that is **blanco**.

Now, trace the word **blanco**.

Name_____

White

Circle the picture that is **blanco** in each row.

Name_____

White

Read the word. Trace the word. Then, write the word on your own.

blanco

blanco	blanco

Color the word **blanco**.

Name_____

White

Which three could be **blanco**?

Color with **blanco**.

Name_____

Color Review

In each row, color two things that are the same color.
Row 1: **rojo**, Row 2: **negro**, and Row 3: **morado**

Name_____

Color Review

In each row, color two things that are the same color.
Row 1: **verde**, Row 2: **amarillo**, and Row 3: **naranja**

Name_____

Color Review

Draw a line to match each picture to the crayon with the same color.

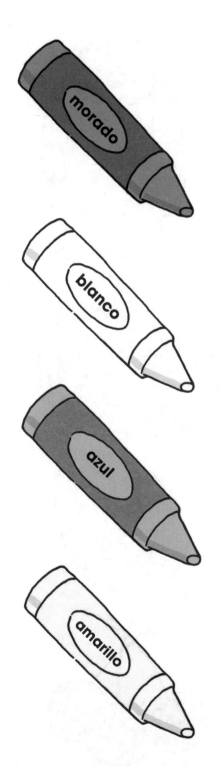

Name_____

Color Review

Draw a line to match each picture to the crayon with the same color.

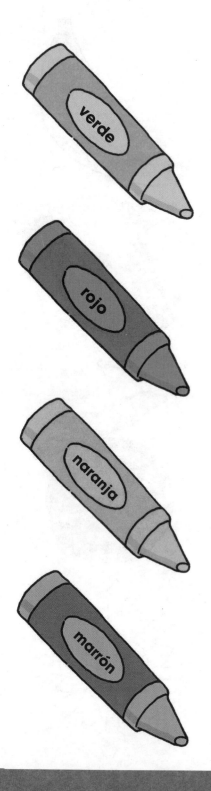

Name_____

Color Review

Color the balloons with the correct colors.

Color **1** balloon **morado**.   Color **2** balloons **verde**.   Color **1** balloon **naranja**.

Color **2** balloons **amarillo**.   Color **1** balloon **azul**.   Color **2** balloons **rojo**.

Name_____

Color Review

Color each picture with the correct crayon.

1	-	rojo
2	-	azul
3	-	amarillo
4	-	verde
5	-	morado
6	-	naranja
7	-	marrón
8	-	negro
9	-	blanco

Name_____

Color Review

Color each space on the palette with the correct crayon. Color the paintbrush, too!

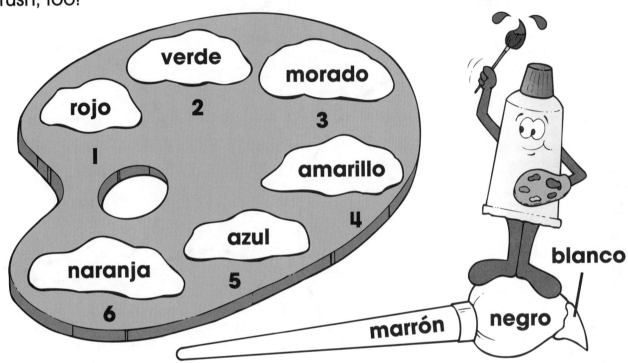

Use each color from the palette to color the pictures. Color the frames to match.

Name_____

Circle

The Spanish word for circle is **círculo**.

Trace the **circles**.

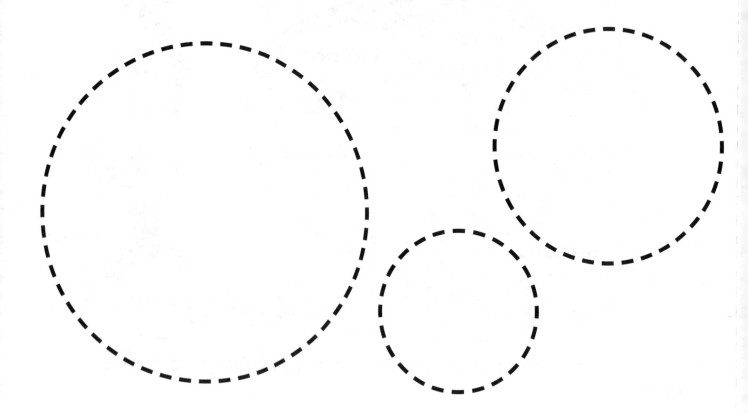

Trace the word.

círculo

Name_____

Circle

This picture has **circles** in it. Trace the **círculos**.

Name_____

Circle

This picture has **circles** in it. Trace the **círculos**.

Name_____

Circle

Color the **círculos**.

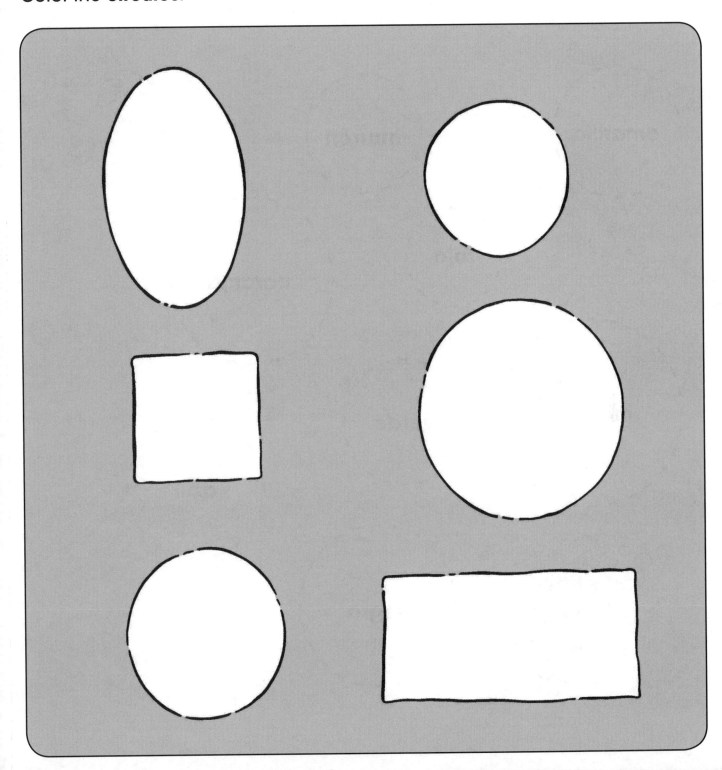

Name_____

Circle

Trace and color each **círculo** with the correct crayon.

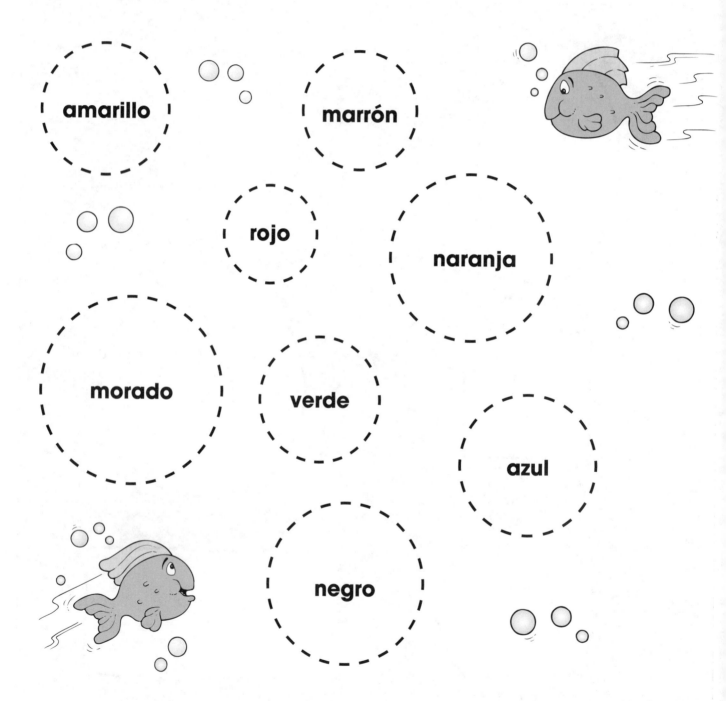

Name_____

Circle

Read the word. Trace the word. Then, write the word on your own.

círculo

círculo   círculo

Name_____

Circle

Practice drawing **círculos**.

Practice writing **círculo** on your own.

Name_____

Square

The Spanish word for square is **cuadrado**.

Trace the **squares**.

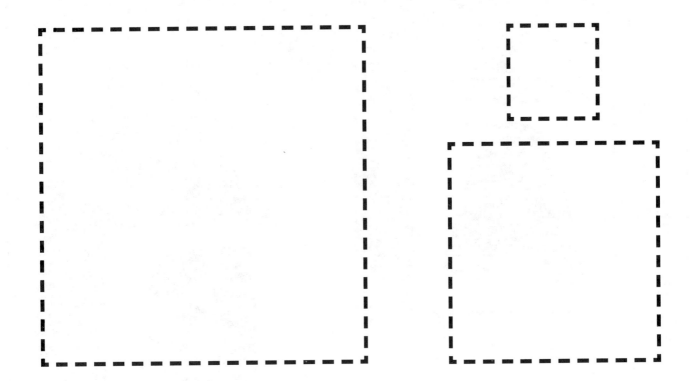

Trace the word.

Name_____

Square

This picture has **squares** in it. Trace the **cuadrados**.

Name_____

Square

This picture has **squares** in it. Trace the **cuadrados**.

Name_____

Square

Color the **cuadrados**.

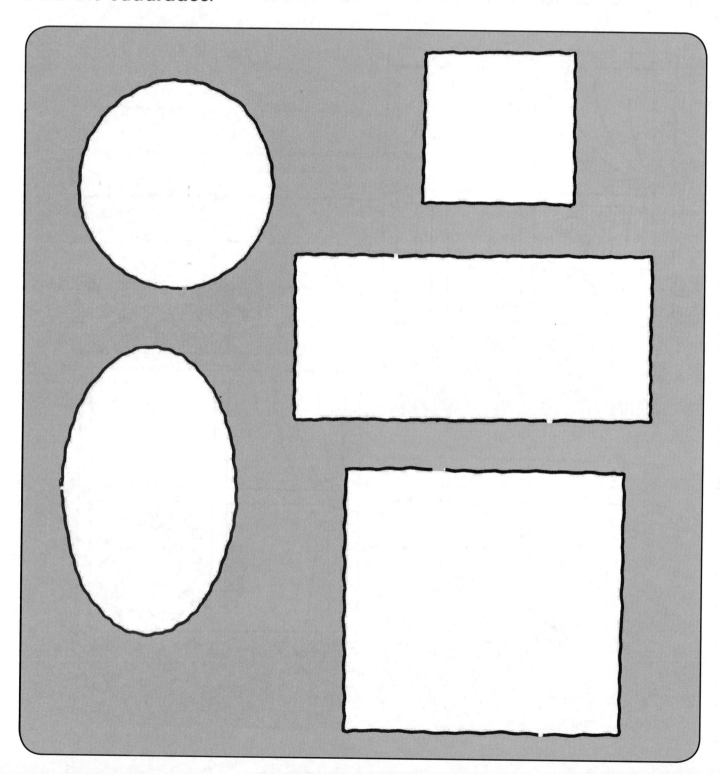

Name_____

Square

Trace and color each **cuadrado** with the correct crayon.

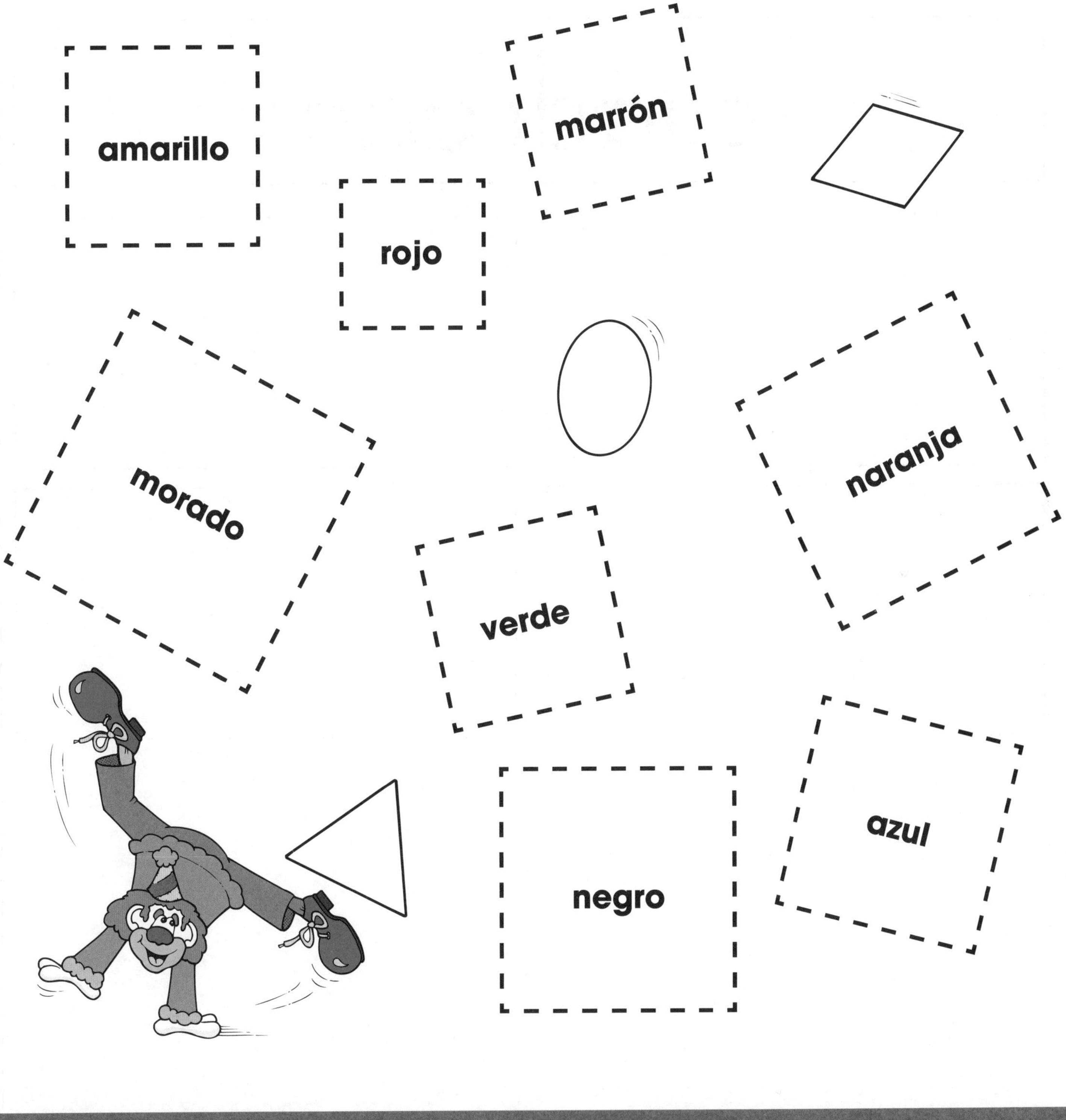

amarillo

marrón

rojo

morado

naranja

verde

azul

negro

Name_____

Square

Read the word. Trace the word. Then, write the word on your own.

cuadrado

cuadrado	cuadrado

Name_____

Square

Practice drawing cuadrados.

Practice writing cuadrado on your own.

Name_____

Triangle

The Spanish word for triangle is **triángulo**.

Trace the **triangles**.

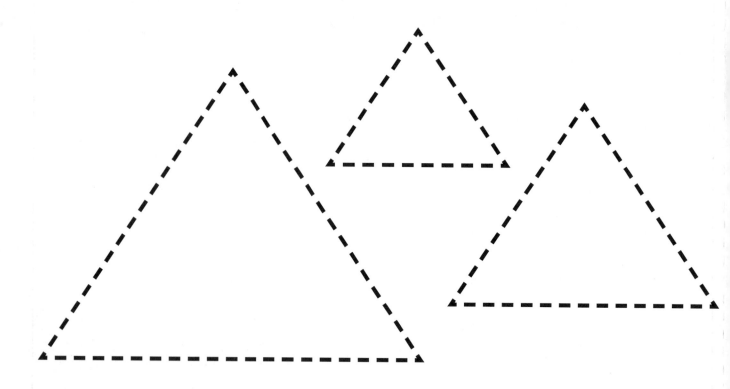

Trace the word.

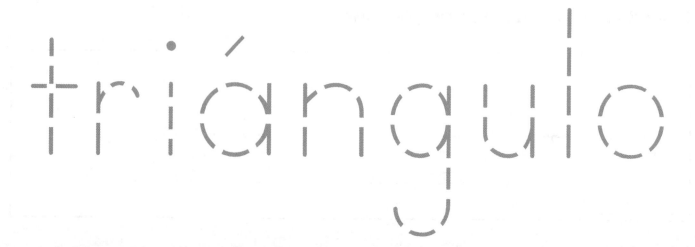

Name_____

Triangle

This picture has **triangles** in it. Trace the **triángulos**.

Name_____

Triangle

This picture has **triangles** in it. Trace the **triángulos**.

Name_____

Triangle

Color the **triángulos**.

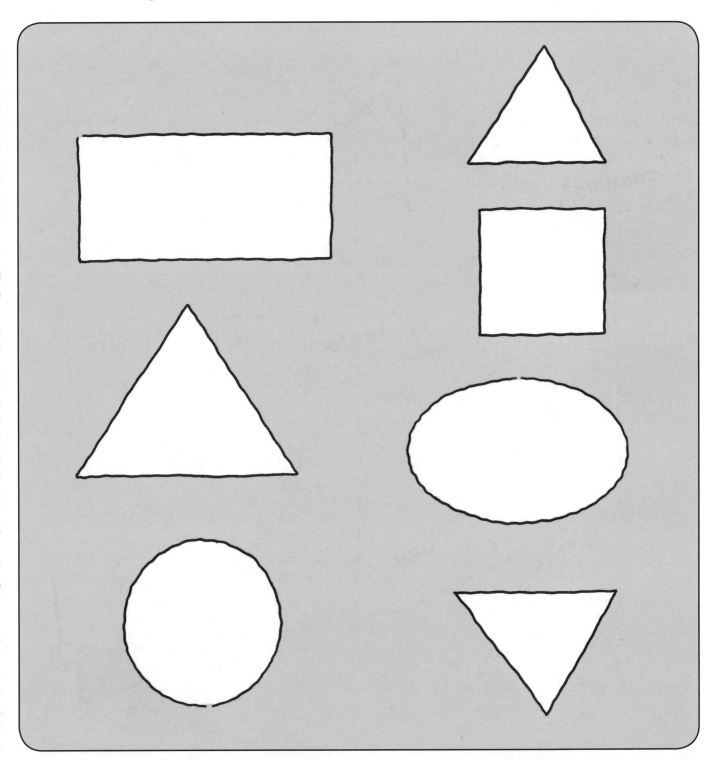

Name_____

Triangle

Trace and color each **triángulo** with the correct crayon.

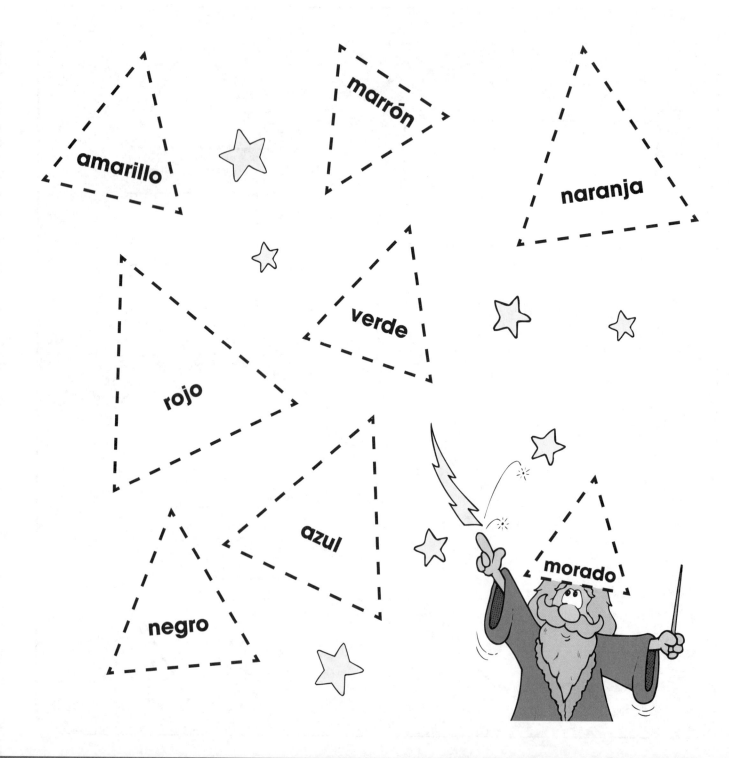

Triangle

Read the word. Trace the word. Then, write the word on your own.

triángulo

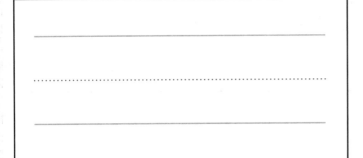

Name_____

Triangle

Practice drawing **triángulos**.

Practice writing **triángulo** on your own.

Name_____

Rectangle

The Spanish word for rectangle is **rectángulo**.

Trace the **rectangles**.

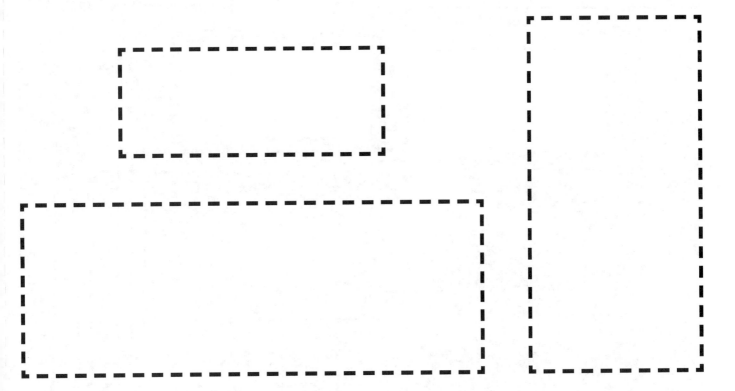

Trace the word.

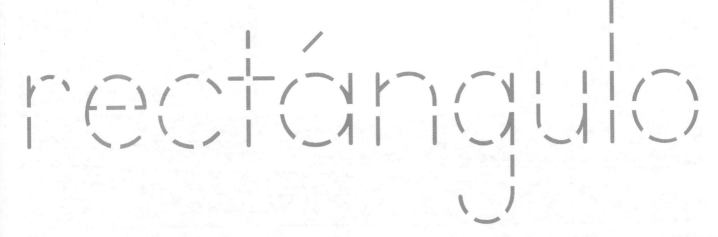

Name_____

Rectangle

This picture has **rectangles** in it. Trace the **rectángulos**.

Name_____

Rectangle

This picture has **rectangles** in it. Trace the **rectángulos**.

Name_____

Rectangle

Color the **rectángulos**.

Name_____

Rectangle

Trace and color each **rectángulo** with the correct crayon.

azul

amarillo

verde

naranja

rojo

negro

morado

Name_____

Rectangle

Read the word. Trace the word. Then, write the word on your own.

rectángulo

rectángulo   rectángulo

Name_____

Rectangle

Practice drawing **rectángulos**.

Practice writing **rectángulo** on your own.

Name_____

Oval

The Spanish word for oval is **óvalo**.

Trace the **ovals**.

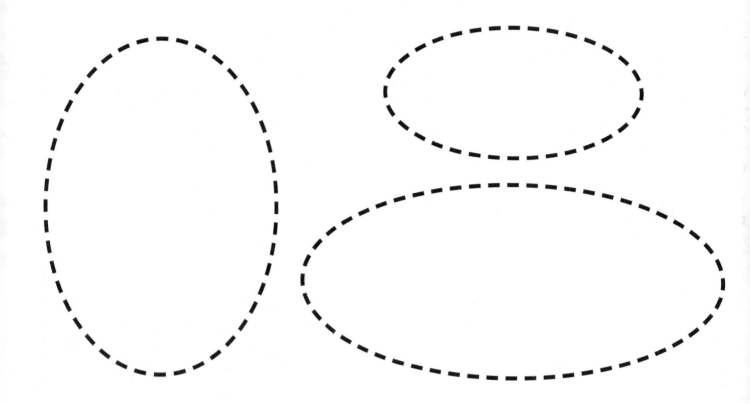

Trace the word.

Name_____

Oval

This picture has **ovals** in it. Trace the **óvalos**.

Name_____

Oval

This picture has **ovals** in it. Trace the **óvalos**.

Name_____

Oval

Color the **óvalos**.

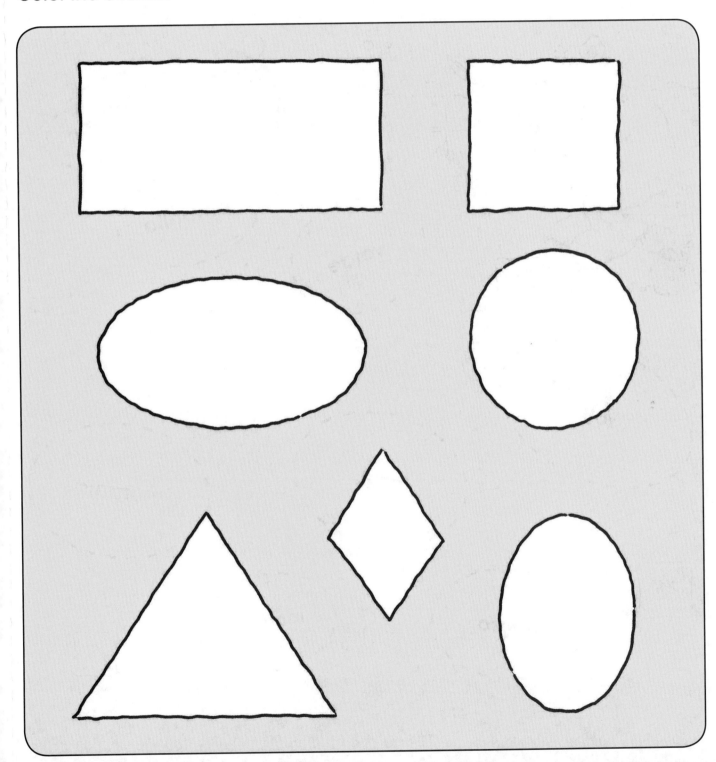

Name_____

Oval

Trace and color each **óvalo** with the correct crayon.

Name_____

Oval

Read the word. Trace the word. Then, write the word on your own.

óvalo

óvalo	óvalo

Name_____

Oval

Practice drawing **óvalos**.

Practice writing **óvalo** on your own.

Name_____

Rhombus

The Spanish word for rhombus is **rombo**.

Trace the **rhombuses**.

Trace the word.

Name_____

Rhombus

This picture has a **rhombus** in it. Trace the **rombo**.

Name_____

Rhombus

This picture has **rhombuses** in it. Trace the **rombos**.

Name_____

Rhombus

Color the **rombos**.

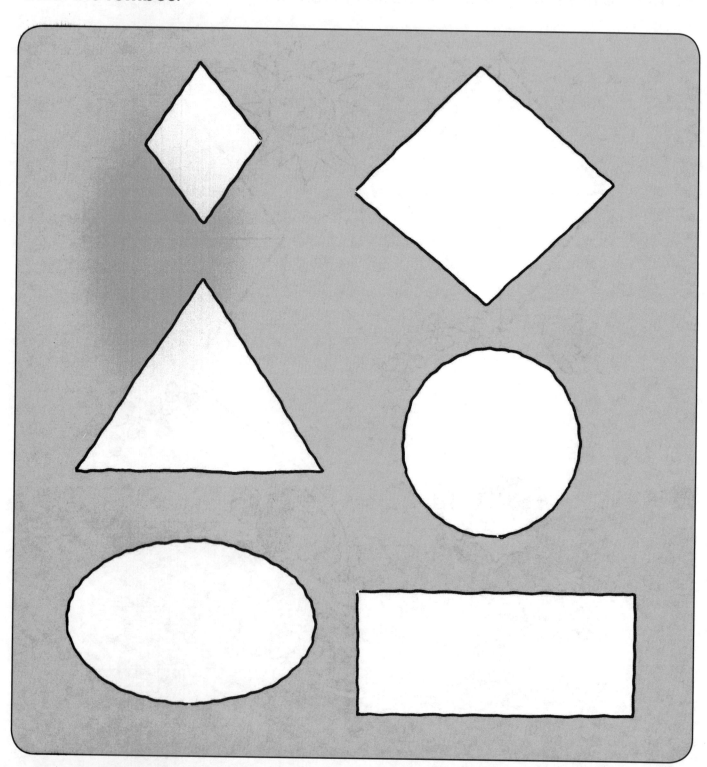

Name_____

Rhombus

Trace and color each **rombo** with the correct crayon.

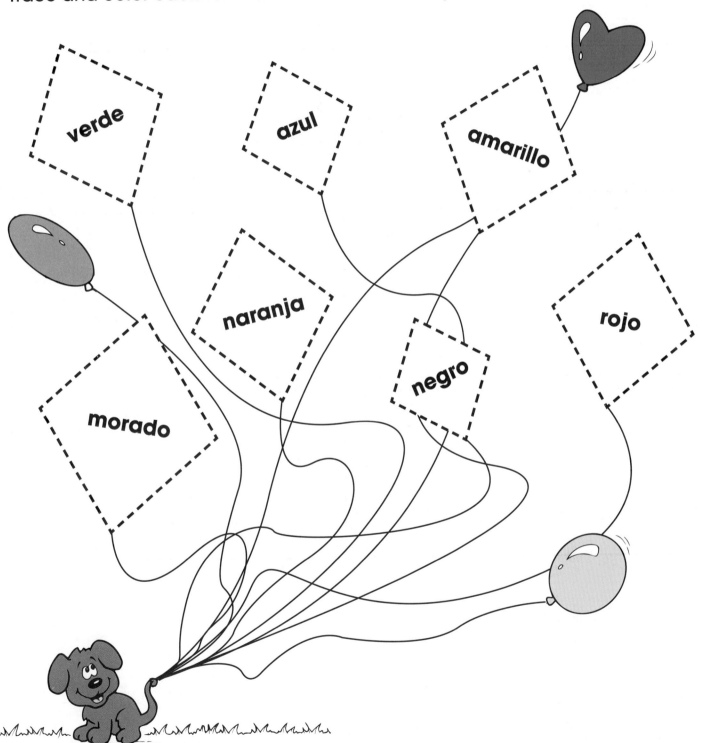

Name_____

Rhombus

Read the word. Trace the word. Then, write the word on your own.

rombo

rombo

rombo

Name_____

Rhombus

Practice drawing **rombos**.

Practice writing **rombo** on your own.

Shape Review

Draw a line to match each shape on the left to the same shape on the right.

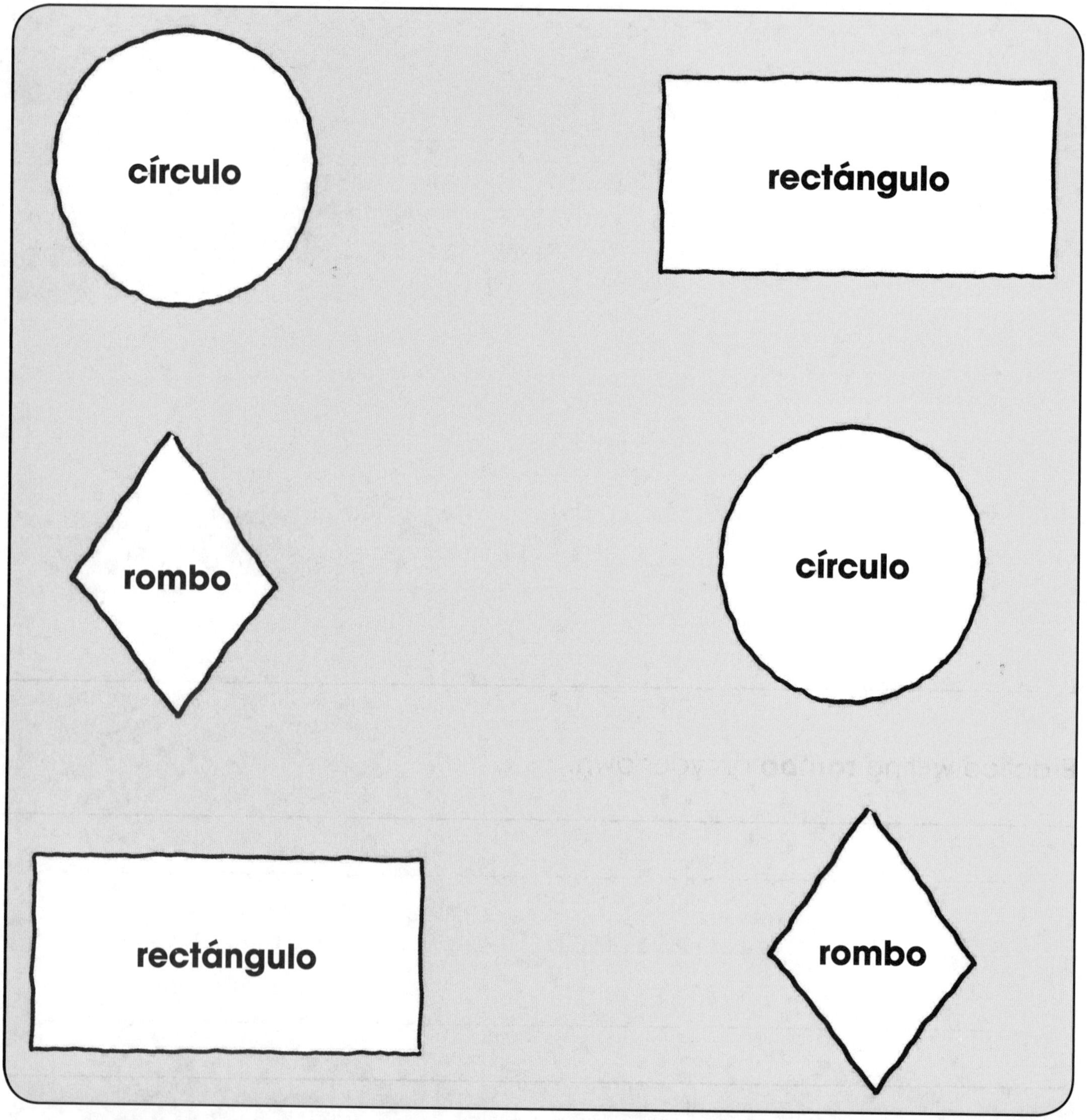

círculo

rectángulo

rombo

círculo

rectángulo

rombo

Name_____

Shape Review

Draw a line to match each shape on the left to a picture with the same shape on the right.

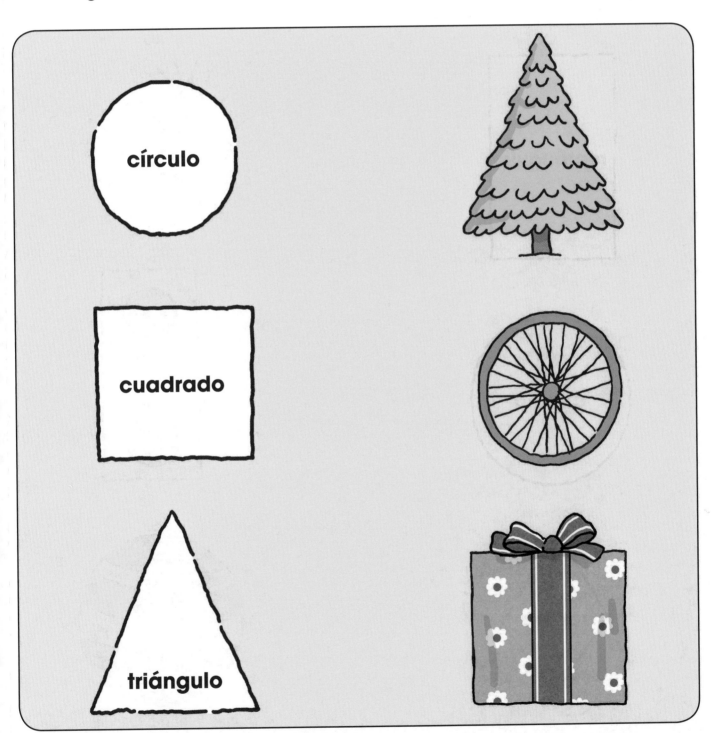

Name_____

Shape Review

Draw a line to match each shape on the left to a picture with the same shape on the right.

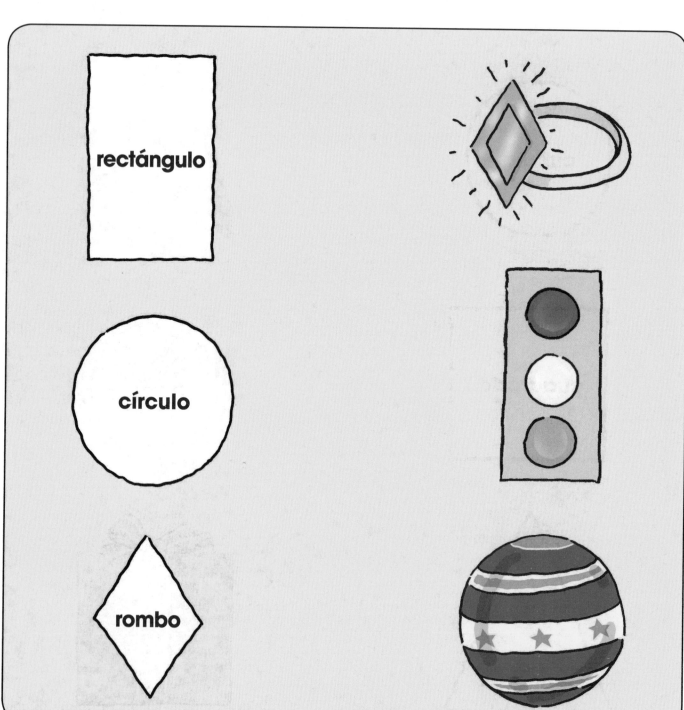

rectángulo

círculo

rombo

Name_____

Shape Review

Color each **cuadrado** blue. Color each **círculo** green. Color each **triángulo** brown. Then, finish the picture with your favorite colors!

Name_____

The Alphabet

Trace the Spanish alphabet.

Name_____

The Alphabet

Say the letters of the Spanish alphabet.

Spanish Letter	Name	Pronunciation
a	a	ah
b	be	bay
c	ce	say
d	de	day
e	e	ay
f	efe	EH-fay
g	ge	hay
h	hache	AH-chay
i	i	ee
j	jota	HOH-ta
k	ka	kah
l	ele	EL-ay
m	eme	EM-ay

Name_____

The Alphabet

Say the letters of the Spanish alphabet.

Spanish Letter	Name	Pronunciation
n	ene	EN-ay
ñ	eñe	EN-yay
o	o	oh
p	pe	pay
q	cu	koo
r	ere	EHR-ay
s	ese	EH-say
t	te	tay
u	u	oo
v	ve	vay
w	doble ve	DOH-blay-vay
x	equis	EH-kees
y	i griega	EE gree-AY-gah
z	zeta	SAY-tah

Name_____

Aa

Trace and write the letter **Aa**. Start at the dot. Say the sound of the Spanish letter **Aa** as you write it.

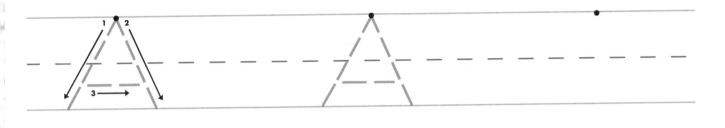

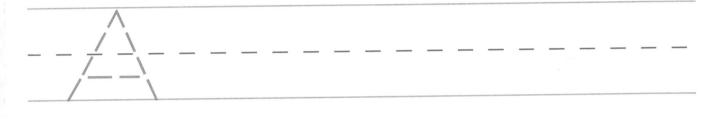

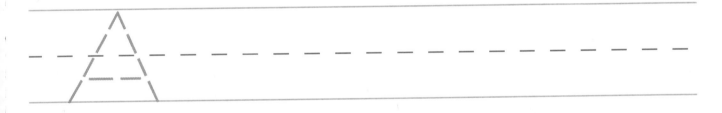

Here is a Spanish word that begins with **Aa**.

abeja
(bee)

Name_____

Aa

Trace and write the letter **Aa**. Start at the dot. Say the sound of the Spanish letter **Aa** as you write it.

Here is a Spanish word that begins with **Aa**.

agua
(water)

Name_____

Bb

Trace and write the letter **Bb**. Start at the dot. Say the sound of the Spanish letter **Bb** as you write it.

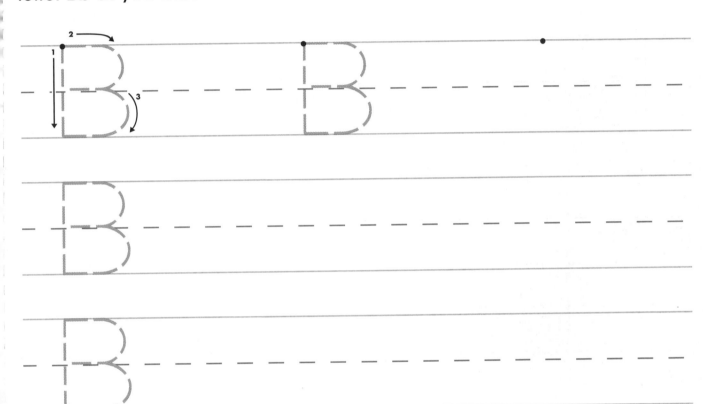

Here is a Spanish word that begins with **Bb**.

**bebé
(baby)**

Name_____

Bb

Trace and write the letter **Bb**. Start at the dot. Say the sound of the Spanish letter **Bb** as you write it.

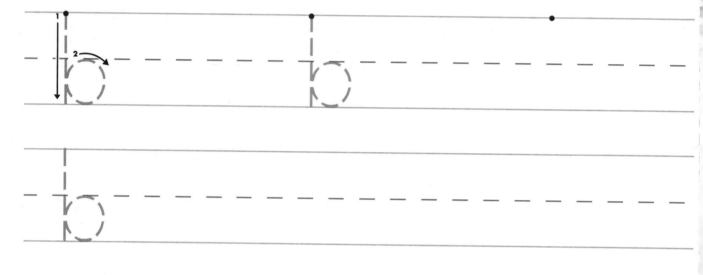

Here is a Spanish word that begins with **Bb**.

bicicleta

(bicycle)

Name_____

Cc

Trace and write the letter **Cc**. Start at the dot. Say the sound of the Spanish letter **Cc** as you write it.

Here is a Spanish word that begins with **Cc**.

**casa
(house)**

Cc

Trace and write the letter **Cc**. Start at the dot. Say the sound of the Spanish letter **Cc** as you write it.

Here is a Spanish word that begins with **Cc**.

**conejo
(rabbit)**

Letter Recognition

Circle the letters in each row that match the first letter.

A	N	A	V	A
a	b	a	c	a
B	B	C	B	A
b	d	a	b	a
C	O	C	D	C
c	a	c	c	o

Name_____

Chch

Trace and write the letter combination **Chch**. Start at the dot. Say the sound of the Spanish letter combination **Chch** (chay) as you write it.

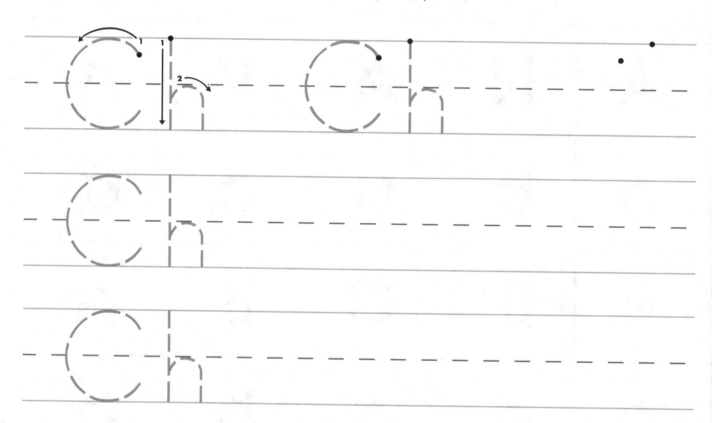

Here is a Spanish word that begins with **Chch**.

**chica
(girl)**

Name_____

Chch

Trace and write the letter combination **Chch**. Start at the dot. Say the sound of the Spanish letter combination **Chch** as you write it.

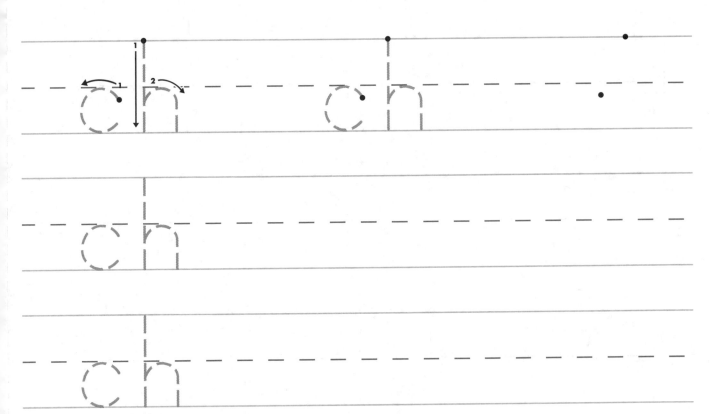

Here is a Spanish word that begins with **Chch**.

**chico
(boy)**

Name_____

Dd

Trace and write the letter **Dd**. Start at the dot. Say the sound of the Spanish letter **Dd** as you write it.

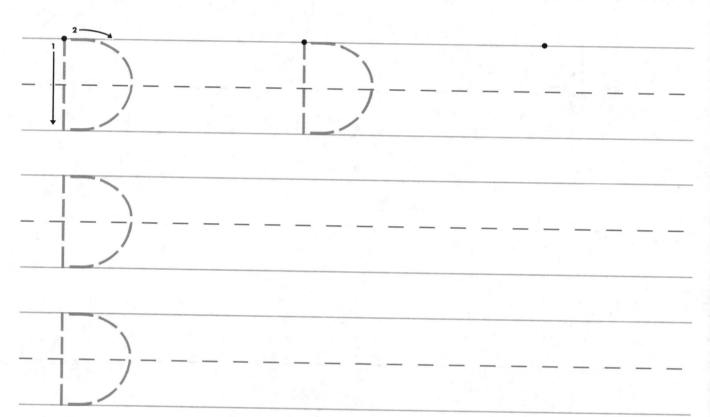

Here is a Spanish word that begins with **Dd**.

**deportes
(sports)**

Name_____

Dd

Trace and write the letter **Dd**. Start at the dot. Say the sound of the Spanish letter **Dd** as you write it.

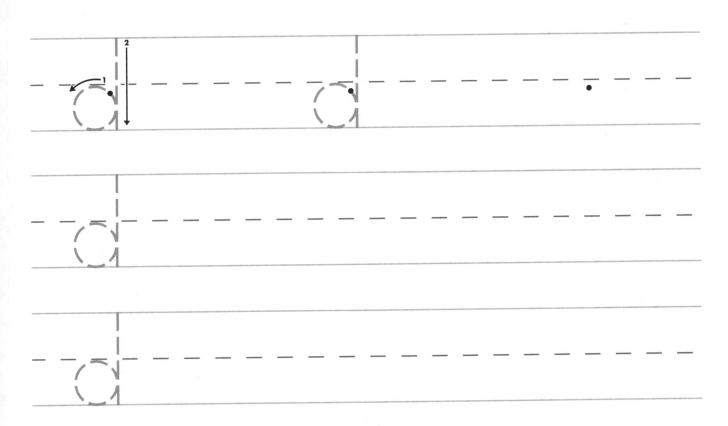

Here is a Spanish word that begins with **Dd**.

**dinero
(money)**

Name_____

Ee

Trace and write the letter **Ee**. Start at the dot. Say the sound of the Spanish letter **Ee** as you write it.

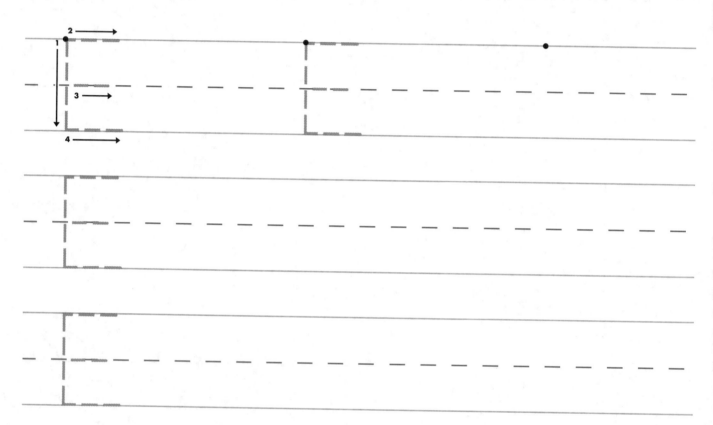

Here is a Spanish word that begins with **Ee**.

**estrella
(star)**

Name_____

Ee

Trace and write the letter **Ee**. Start at the dot. Say the sound of the Spanish letter **Ee** as you write it.

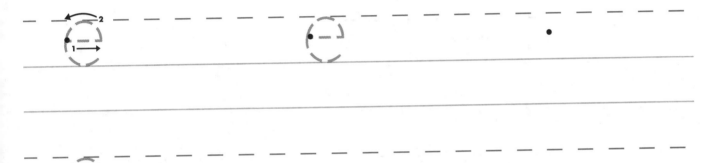

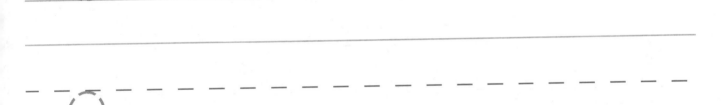

Here is a Spanish word that begins with **Ee**.

**espejo
(mirror)**

Ff

Trace and write the letter **Ff**. Start at the dot. Say the sound of the Spanish letter **Ff** as you write it.

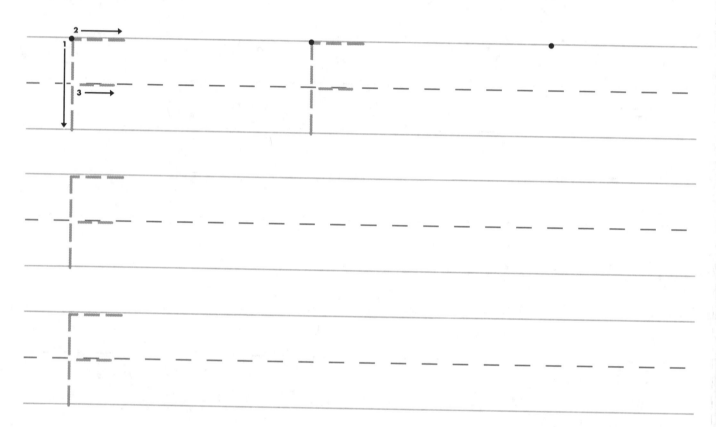

Here is a Spanish word that begins with **Ff**.

fiesta

(party)

Name_____

Ff

Trace and write the letter **Ff**. Start at the dot. Say the sound of the Spanish letter **Ff** as you write it.

Here is a Spanish word that begins with **Ff**.

flor
(flower)

Letter Recognition

Circle the letters in each row that match the first letter.

D	**B**	**G**	**D**	**B**
d	**b**	**d**	**a**	**d**
E	**H**	**F**	**E**	**E**
e	**e**	**a**	**b**	**e**
F	**E**	**F**	**E**	**A**
f	**t**	**f**	**l**	**o**

Name_____

Gg

Trace and write the letter **Gg**. Start at the dot. Say the sound of the Spanish letter **Gg** as you write it.

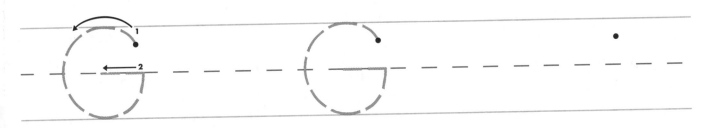

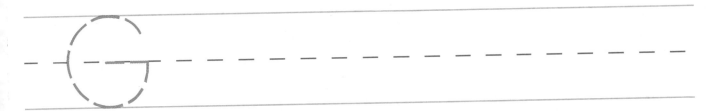

Here is a Spanish word that begins with **Gg**.

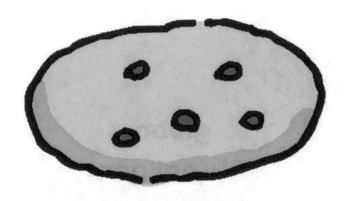

galleta (cookie)

Gg

Trace and write the letter **Gg**. Start at the dot. Say the sound of the Spanish letter **Gg** as you write it.

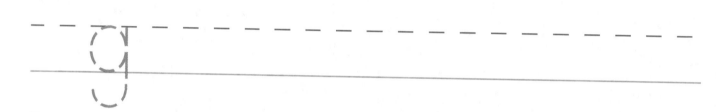

Here is a Spanish word that begins with **Gg**.

globo
(balloon)

Name_____

Hh

Trace and write the letter **Hh**. Start at the dot. Say the sound of the Spanish letter **Hh** as you write it.

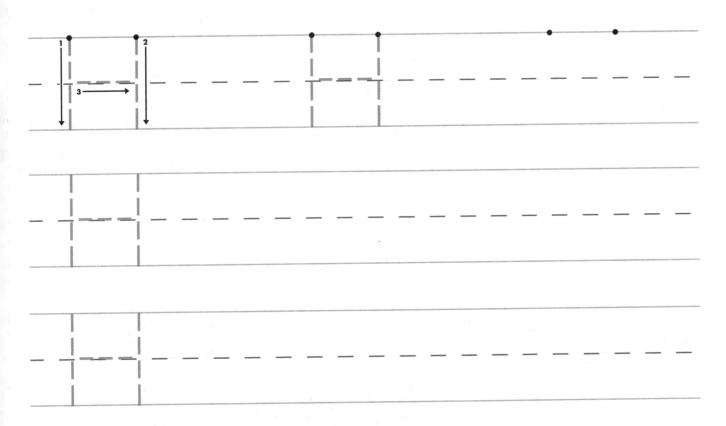

Here is a Spanish word that begins with **Hh**.

**hombre
(man)**

Name_____

Hh

Trace and write the letter **Hh**. Start at the dot. Say the sound of the Spanish letter **Hh** as you write it.

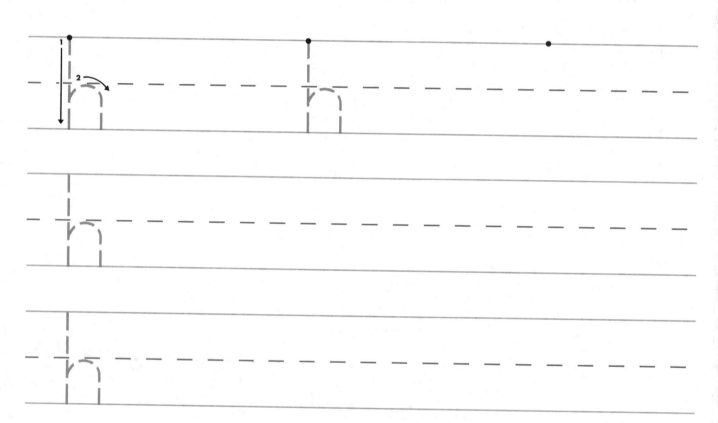

Here is a Spanish word that begins with **Hh**.

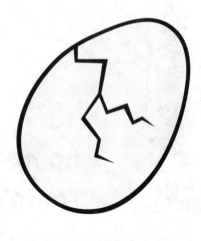

huevo
(egg)

Name_____

Ii

Trace and write the letter **Ii**. Start at the dot. Say the sound of the Spanish letter **Ii** as you write it.

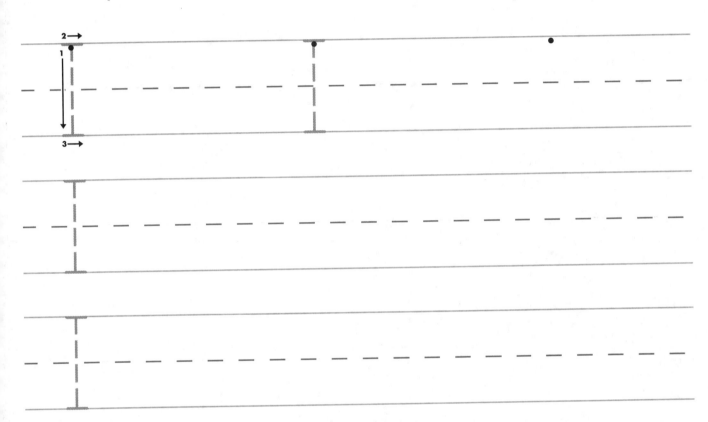

Here is a Spanish word that begins with **Ii**.

insecto
(insect)

Ii

Trace and write the letter **Ii**. Start at the dot. Say the sound of the Spanish letter **Ii** as you write it.

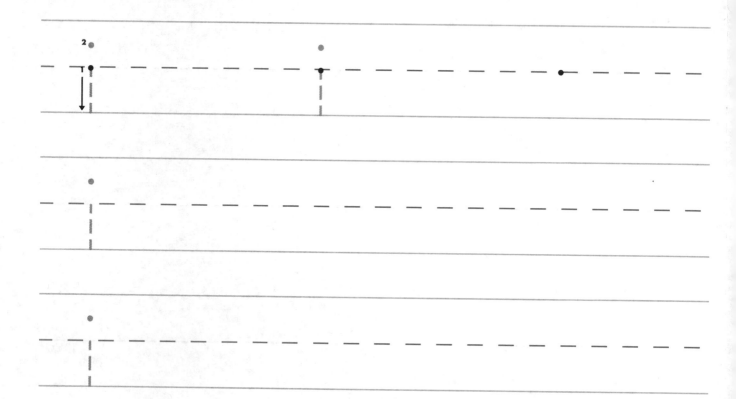

Here is a Spanish word that begins with **Ii**.

isla

(island)

Name_____

Letter Recognition

Circle the letters in each row that match the first letter.

G	C	G	O	B
g	g	p	q	g
H	E	F	H	I
h	d	n	b	h
I	H	I	L	A
i	t	i	l	i

Name_____

Jj

Trace and write the letter **Jj**. Start at the dot. Say the sound of the Spanish letter **Jj** as you write it.

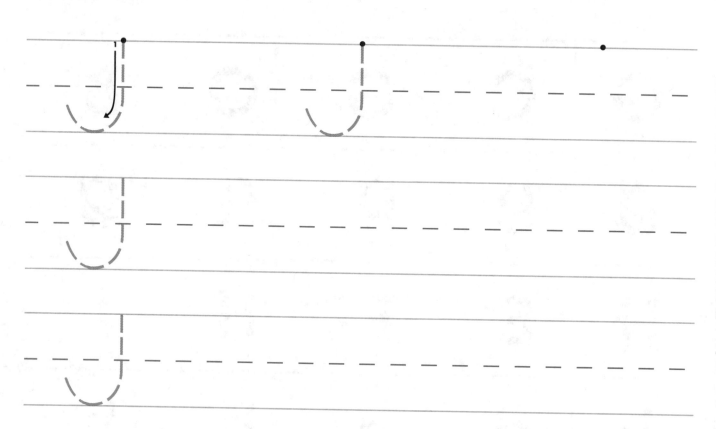

Here is a Spanish word that begins with **Jj**.

jabón
(soap)

Name_____

Jj

Trace and write the letter **Jj**. Start at the dot. Say the sound of the Spanish letter **Jj** as you write it.

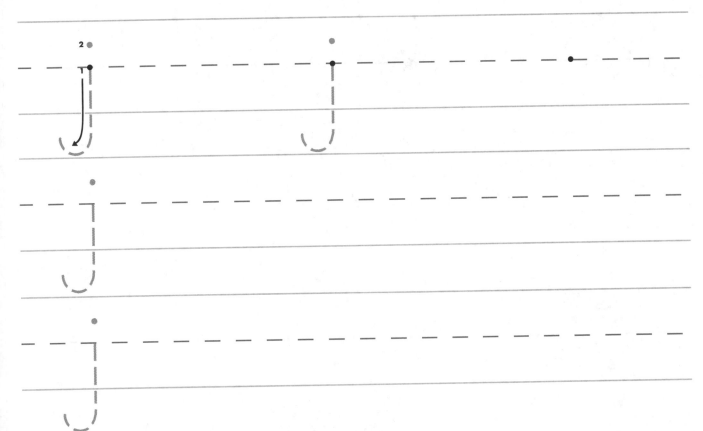

Here is a Spanish word that begins with **Jj**.

juego
(game)

Name_____

Kk

Trace and write the letter **Kk**. Start at the dot. Say the sound of the Spanish letter **Kk** as you write it.

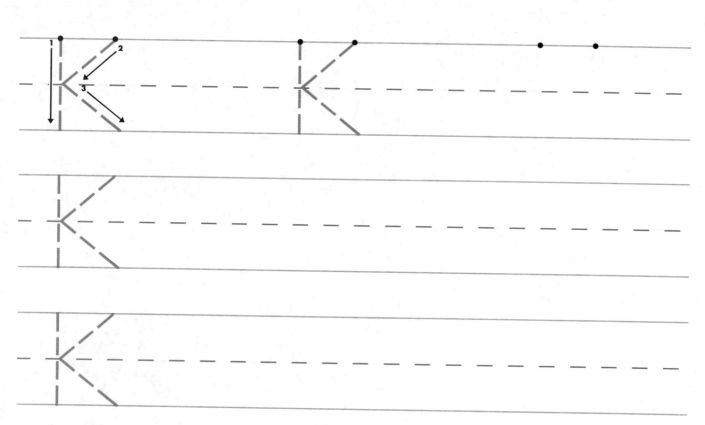

Here is a Spanish word that begins with **Kk**.

karate

(karate)

Name_____

Kk

Trace and write the letter **Kk**. Start at the dot. Say the sound of the Spanish letter **Kk** as you write it.

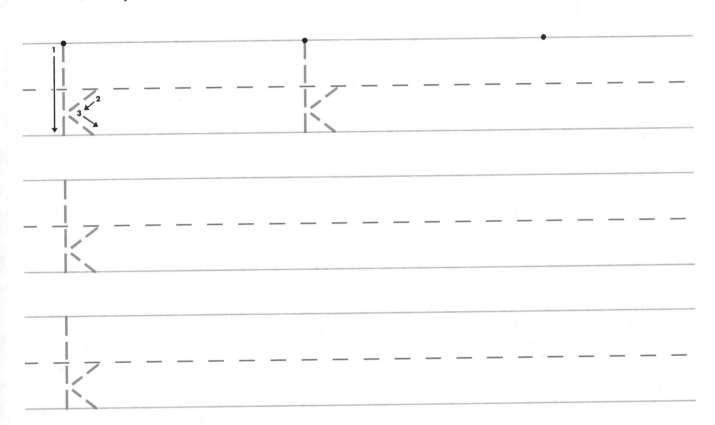

Here is a Spanish word that begins with **Kk**.

koala
(koala)

Name_____

Ll

Trace and write the letter **Ll**. Start at the dot. Say the sound of the Spanish letter **Ll** as you write it.

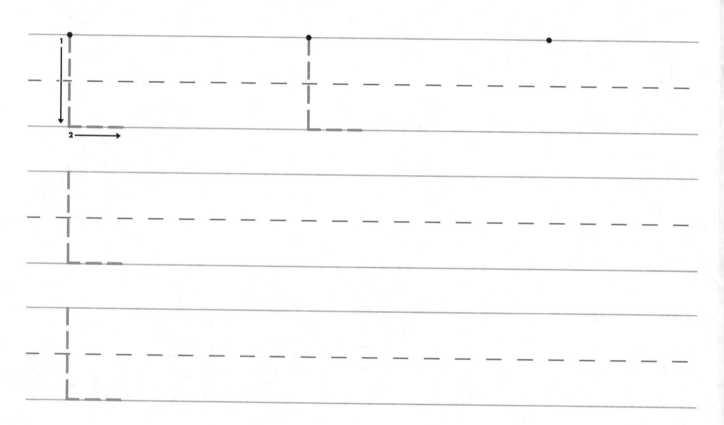

Here is a Spanish word that begins with **Ll**.

libro
(book)

Name_____

Ll

Trace and write the letter **Ll**. Start at the dot. Say the sound of the Spanish letter **Ll** as you write it.

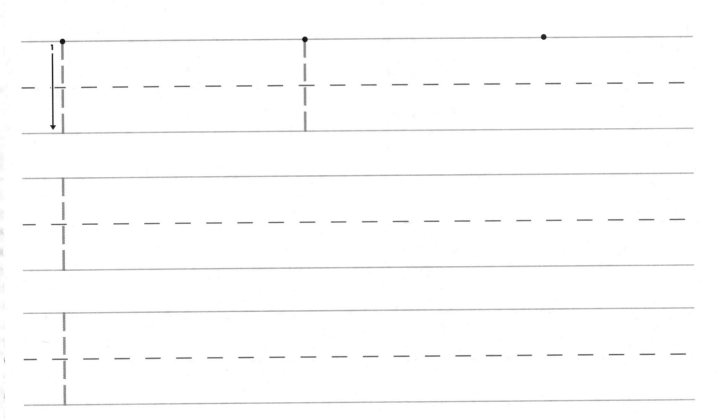

Here is a Spanish word that begins with **Ll**.

luna
(moon)

Name_____

ll

Trace and write the letter combination **ll**. Start at the dot. Say the sound of the Spanish letter combination **ll** (EH-lyay) as you write it.

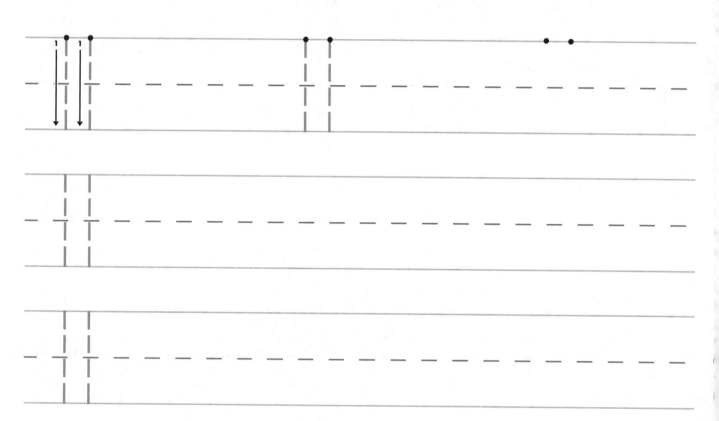

Here is a Spanish word that begins with **ll**.

llave
(key)

Name_____

ll

Trace and write the letter combination **ll**. Start at the dot. Say the sound of the Spanish letter combination **ll** as you write it.

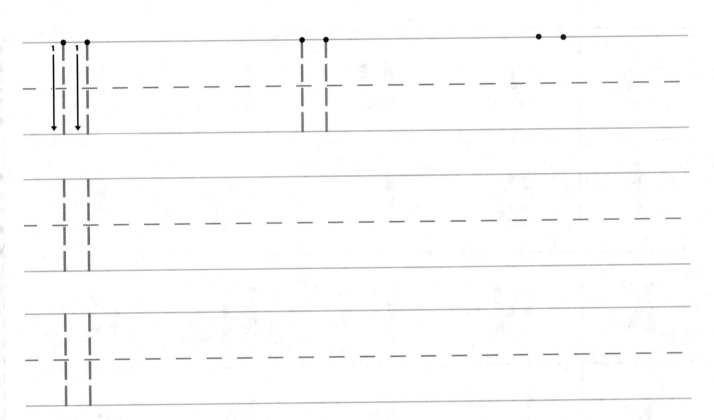

Here is a Spanish word that begins with **ll**.

lluvia
(rain)

Name_____

Letter Recognition

Circle the letters in each row that match the first letter.

J	J	U	L	J
j	g	j	q	i
K	N	F	H	K
k	l	h	k	b
L	J	I	L	U
I	t	i	l	i

Name_____

Mm

Trace and write the letter **Mm**. Start at the dot. Say the sound of the Spanish letter **Mm** as you write it.

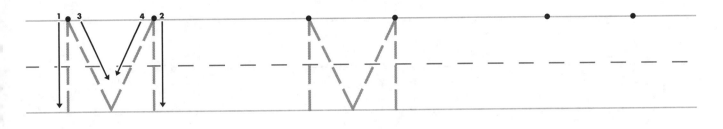

Here is a Spanish word that begins with **Mm**.

manzana
(apple)

Name_____

Mm

Trace and write the letter **Mm**. Start at the dot. Say the sound of the Spanish letter **Mm** as you write it.

Here is a Spanish word that begins with **Mm**.

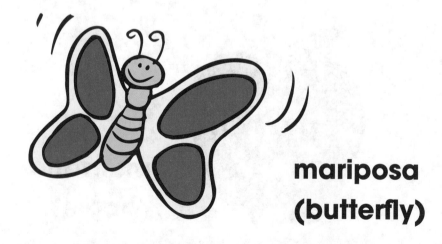

**mariposa
(butterfly)**

Nn

Trace and write the letter **Nn**. Start at the dot. Say the sound of the Spanish letter **Nn** as you write it.

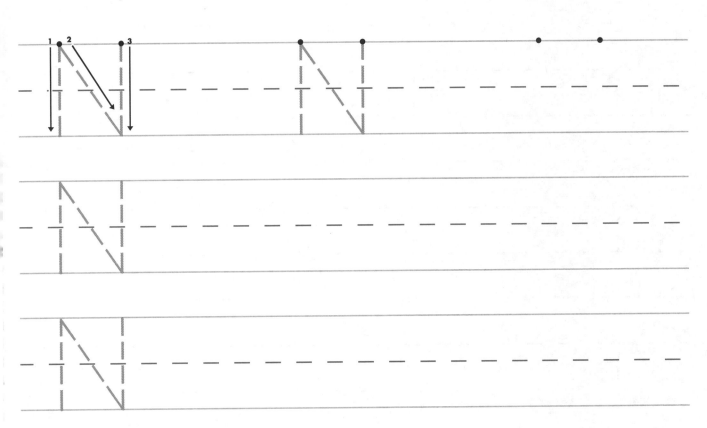

Here is a Spanish word that begins with **Nn**.

nido
(nest)

Name_____

Nn

Trace and write the letter **Nn**. Start at the dot. Say the sound of the Spanish letter **Nn** as you write it.

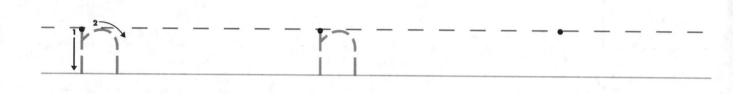

Here is a Spanish word that begins with **Nn**.

nube
(cloud)

Name_____

Ññ

Trace and write the letter **Ññ**. Start at the dot. Say the sound of the Spanish letter **Ññ** as you write it.

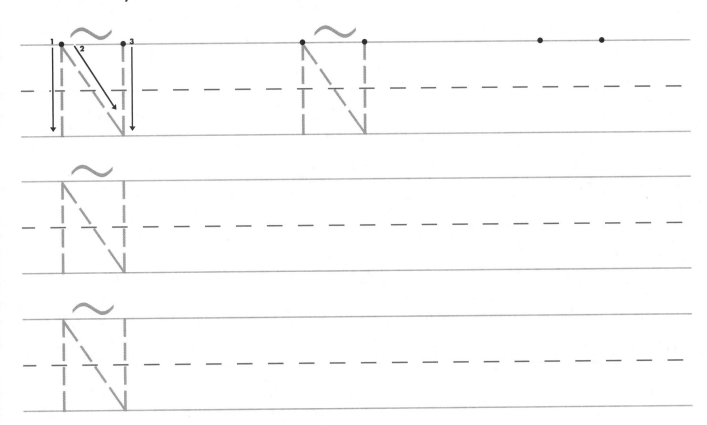

Here is a Spanish word with **Ññ** in it.

niña
(girl child)

Ññ

Trace and write the letter **Ññ**. Start at the dot. Say the sound of the Spanish letter **Ññ** as you write it.

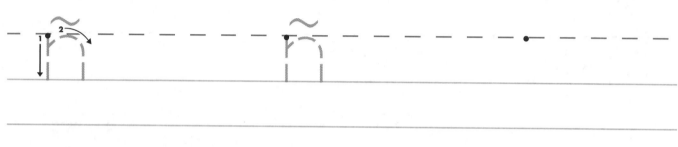

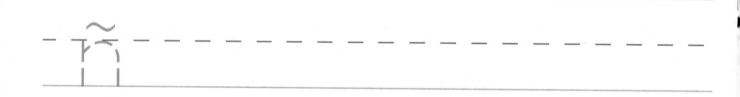

Here is a Spanish word with **Ññ** in it.

niño
(boy child)

Name_____

Oo

Trace and write the letter **Oo**. Start at the dot. Say the sound of the Spanish letter **Oo** as you write it.

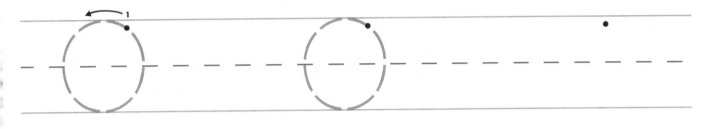

Here is a Spanish word that begins with **Oo**.

océano
(ocean)

Name_____

Oo

Trace and write the letter **Oo**. Start at the dot. Say the sound of the Spanish letter **Oo** as you write it.

Here is a Spanish word that begins with **Oo**.

oso
(bear)

Name_____

Letter Recognition

Circle the letters in each row that match the first letter.

M	H	M	n	L
m	M	a	m	n
N	M	N	m	N
n	n	m	a	n
O	O	D	B	O
o	a	O	c	o

Name_____

Pp

Trace and write the letter **Pp**. Start at the dot. Say the sound of the Spanish letter **Pp** as you write it.

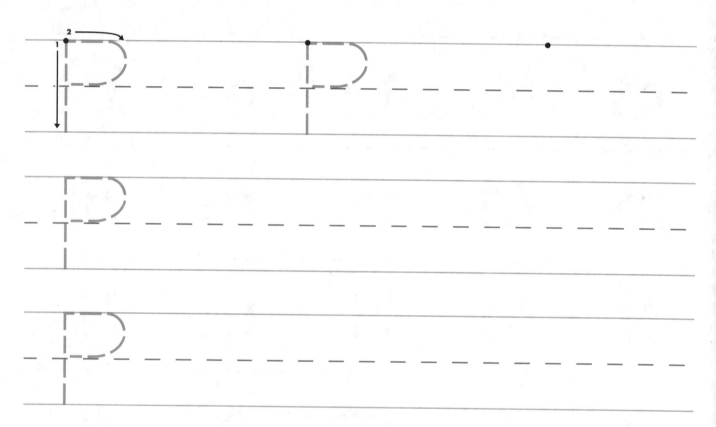

Here is a Spanish word that begins with **Pp**.

pelota
(ball)

Name_____

Pp

Trace and write the letter **Pp**. Start at the dot. Say the sound of the Spanish letter **Pp** as you write it.

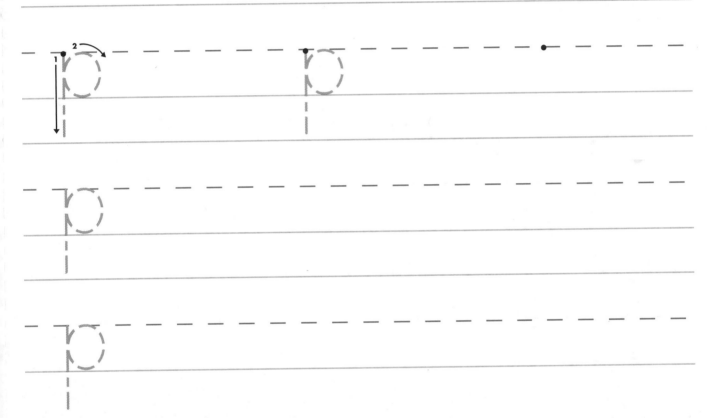

Here is a Spanish word that begins with **Pp**.

pez
(fish)

Name_____

Qq

Trace and write the letter **Qq**. Start at the dot. Say the sound of the Spanish letter **Qq** as you write it.

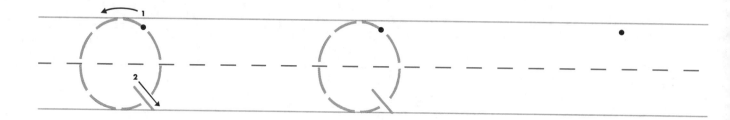

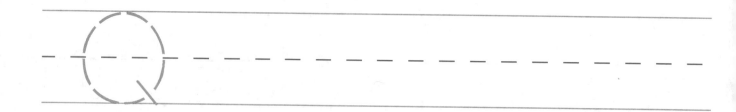

Here is a Spanish word that begins with **Qq**.

quince
(fifteen)

Name_____

Qq

Trace and write the letter **Qq**. Start at the dot. Say the sound of the Spanish letter **Qq** as you write it.

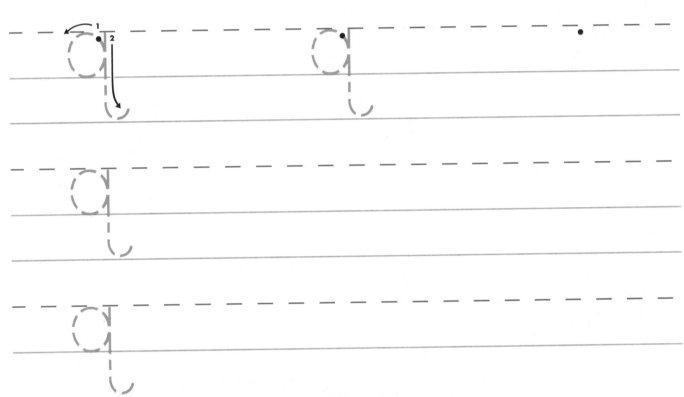

Here is a Spanish word that begins with **Qq**.

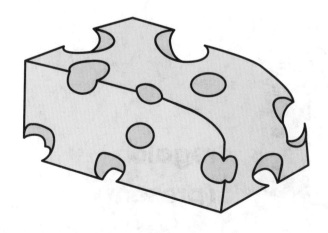

**queso
(cheese)**

Name_____

Rr

Trace and write the letter **Rr**. Start at the dot. Say the sound of the Spanish letter **Rr** as you write it.

Here is a Spanish word that begins with **Rr**.

**regalo
(present)**

Name_____

Rr

Trace and write the letter **Rr**. Start at the dot. Say the sound of the Spanish letter **Rr** as you write it.

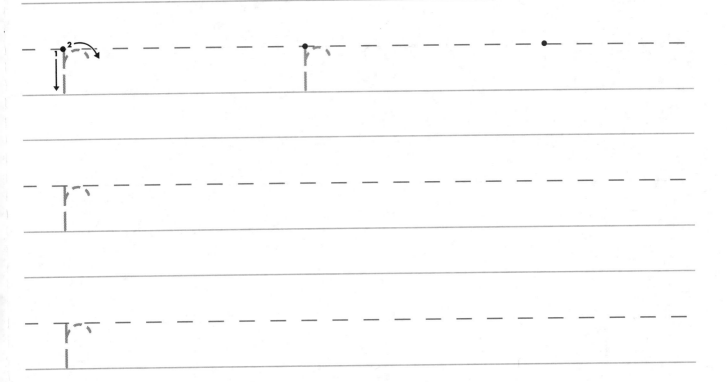

Here is a Spanish word that begins with **Rr**.

rosa
(rose)

Name_____

rr

Trace and write the letter combination **rr**. Start at the dot. Say the sound of the Spanish letter combination **rr** (EHRR-ay) as you write it.

Here is a Spanish word that has **rr** in it.

**perro
(dog)**

Name_____

rr

Trace and write the letter combination **rr**. Start at the dot. Say the sound of the Spanish letter combination **rr** as you write it.

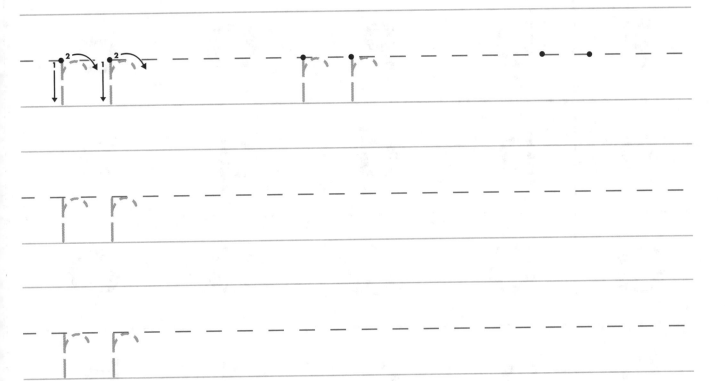

Here is a Spanish word that has **rr** in it.

arroz
(rice)

Name_____

Letter Recognition

Circle the letters in each row that match the first letter.

P	D	P	O	b
p	p	d	q	b
Q	O	Q	G	Q
q	p	q	d	b
R	R	B	P	R
r	r	n	m	r

Name_____

Ss

Trace and write the letter **Ss**. Start at the dot. Say the sound of the Spanish letter **Ss** as you write it.

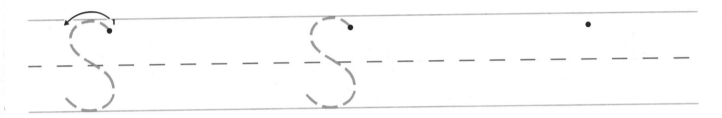

Here is a Spanish word that begins with **Ss**.

**señora
(lady)**

Name_____

Ss

Trace and write the letter **Ss**. Start at the dot. Say the sound of the Spanish letter **Ss** as you write it.

Here is a Spanish word that begins with **Ss**.

sopa
(soup)

Name_____

Tt

Trace and write the letter **Tt**. Start at the dot. Say the sound of the Spanish letter **Tt** as you write it.

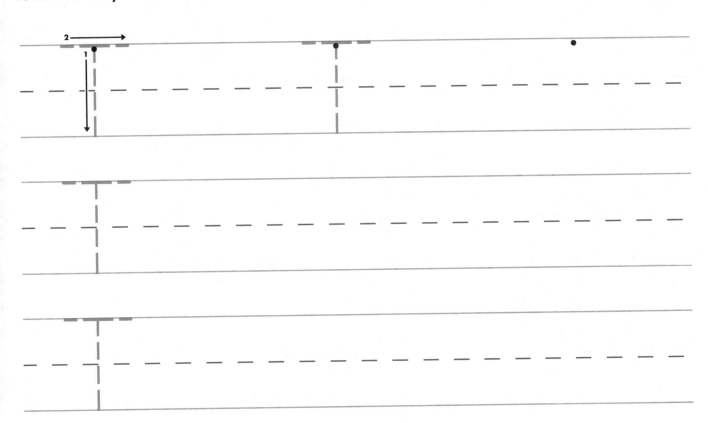

Here is a Spanish word that begins with **Tt**.

tijeras
(scissors)

Tt

Trace and write the letter **Tt**. Start at the dot. Say the sound of the Spanish letter **Tt** as you write it.

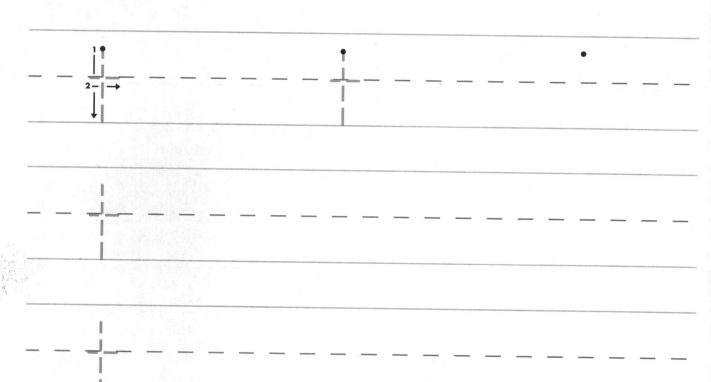

Here is a Spanish word that begins with **Tt**.

tren
(train)

Name_____

Uu

Trace and write the letter **Uu**. Start at the dot. Say the sound of the Spanish letter **Uu** as you write it.

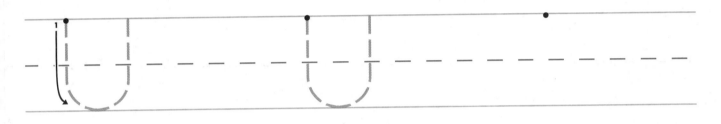

Here is a Spanish word that begins with **Uu**.

uvas
(grapes)

Name_____

Uu

Trace and write the letter **Uu**. Start at the dot. Say the sound of the Spanish letter **Uu** as you write it.

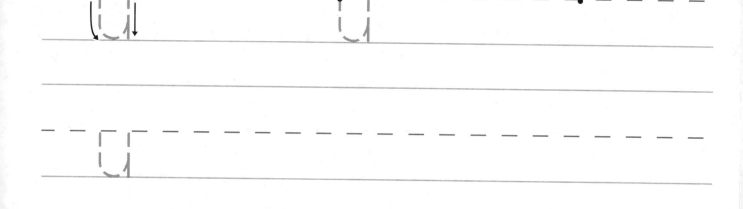

Here is a Spanish word that begins with **Uu**.

1

uno
(one)

Name_____

Letter Recognition

Circle the letters in each row that match the first letter.

S	P	S	B	S
s	o	a	s	e
T	I	P	L	T
t	f	l	t	i
U	U	D	U	O
u	u	n	m	n

Name_____

Vv

Trace and write the letter **Vv**. Start at the dot. Say the sound of the Spanish letter **Vv** as you write it.

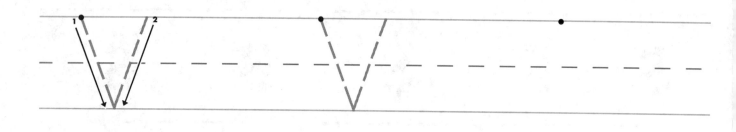

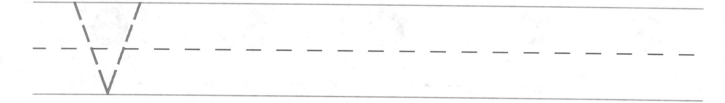

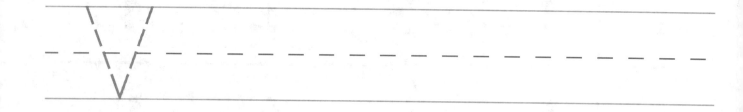

Here is a Spanish word that begins with **Vv**.

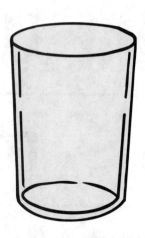

vaso
(glass)

Vv

Trace and write the letter **Vv**. Start at the dot. Say the sound of the Spanish letter **Vv** as you write it.

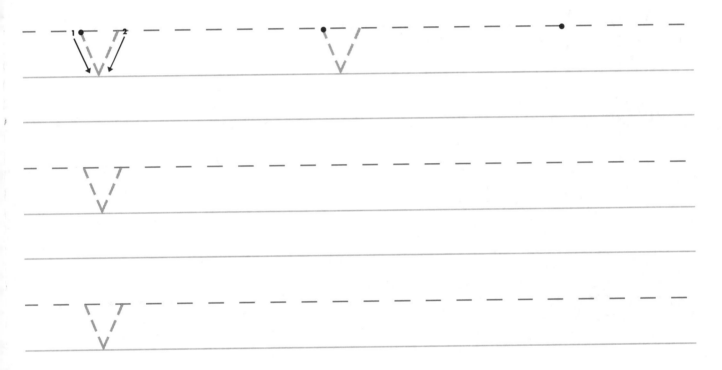

Here is a Spanish word that begins with **Vv**.

**ventana
(window)**

Name_____

Ww

Trace and write the letter **Ww**. Start at the dot. Say the sound of the Spanish letter **Ww** as you write it.

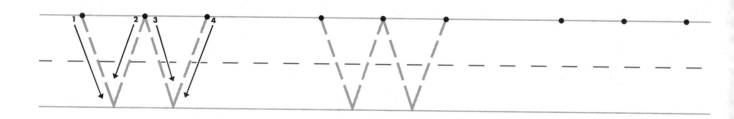

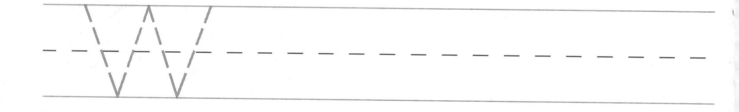

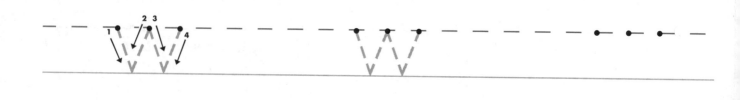

Here is a Spanish word that begins with **Ww**.

watt

(watt)

Name_____

Xx

Trace and write the letter **Xx**. Start at the dot. Say the sound of the Spanish letter **Xx** as you write it.

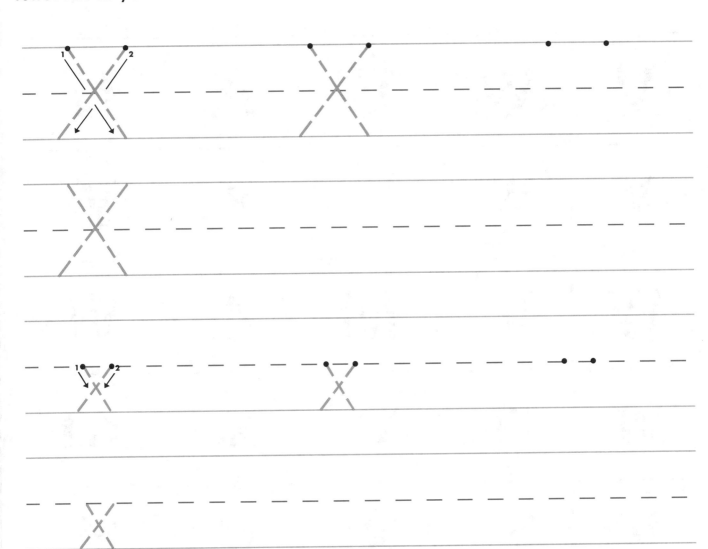

Here is a Spanish word that begins with **Xx**.

xilófone
(xylophone)

Letter Recognition

Circle the letters in each row that match the first letter.

V	W	V	A	N
v	w	x	v	y
W	V	M	A	W
w	w	v	x	m
X	Y	X	V	K
x	y	k	x	z

Name_____

Yy

Trace and write the letter **Yy**. Start at the dot. Say the sound of the Spanish letter **Yy** as you write it.

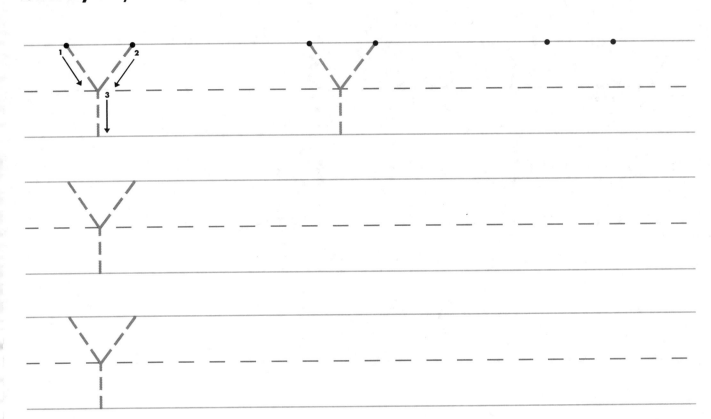

Here is a Spanish word that begins with **Yy**.

**yogur
(yogurt)**

Yy

Trace and write the letter **Yy**. Start at the dot. Say the sound of the Spanish letter **Yy** as you write it.

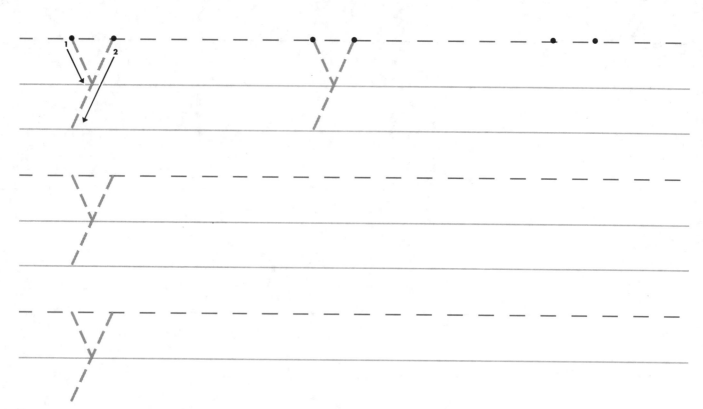

Here is a Spanish word that begins with **Yy**.

yema
(yolk)

Zz

Trace and write the letter **Zz**. Start at the dot. Say the sound of the Spanish letter **Zz** as you write it.

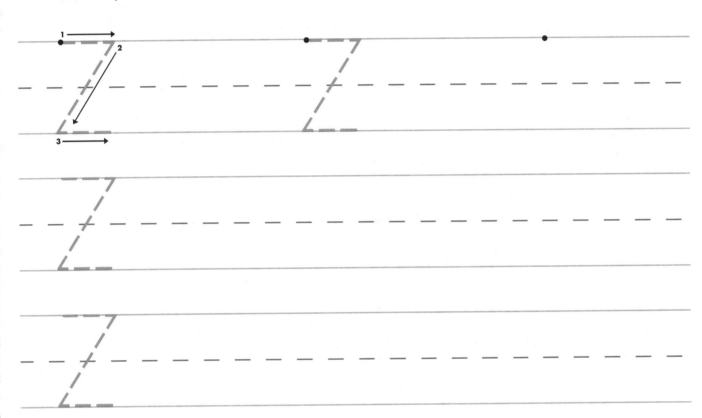

Here is a Spanish word that begins with **Zz**.

zorro

(fox)

Name_____

Zz

Trace and write the letter **Zz**. Start at the dot. Say the sound of the Spanish letter **Zz** as you write it.

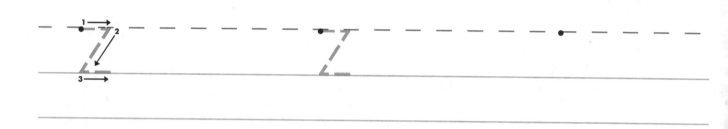

Here is a Spanish word that begins with **Zz**.

**zoológico
(zoo)**

Name_____

Letter Recognition

Circle the letters in each row that match the first letter.

Y	W	Y	V	X
y	w	x	v	y
Z	N	M	Z	W
z	n	z	x	m

Name_____

Alphabet Review: Uppercase

Trace the uppercase letters. Write the missing uppercase letters.

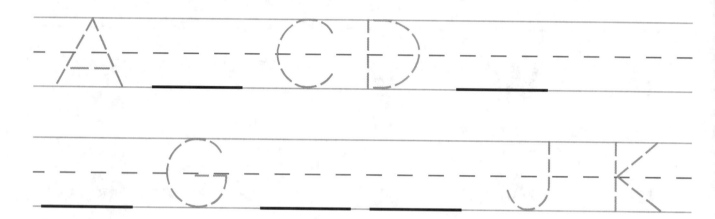

A __ __ C D __ __

__ __ G __ __ J K

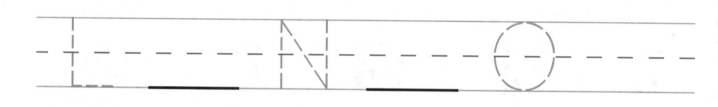

L __ __ N __ O __ __

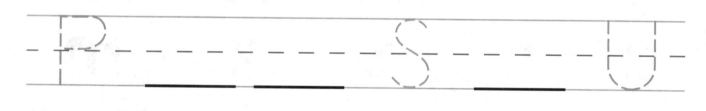

P __ __ __ S __ U __

W __ Y __

Name_____

Alphabet Review: Lowercase

Trace the lowercase letters. Write the missing lowercase letters.

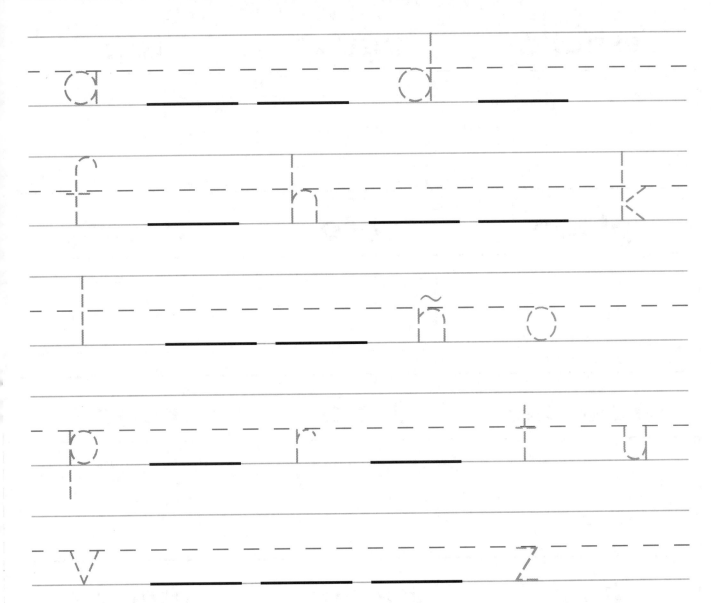

a ____ ____ a ____

f ____ h ____ ____ k

i ____ ____ ñ o

p ____ r ____ t u

v ____ ____ ____ z

Name_____

ABC Order

Put the Spanish words in **abc** order.

estrella   agua   isla

globo   vaso   queso

mariposa   zorro   nube

luna   huevo   dinero

Name_____

ABC Order

Put the Spanish words in **abc** order.

sopa	**tren**	**regalo**

niño	**uvas**	**libro**

señora	**chica**	**niña**

espejo	**bebé**	**juego**

Name_____

ABC Order

Put the Spanish words in **abc** order.

casa	bicicleta	abeja

pelota	fiesta	insecto

ventana	rosa	tijeras

yema	pez	chico

Name_____

Classroom Words

Answer each question with the correct Spanish word.

1. What do you read?
2. What do you cut with?
3. What do you write with?

lápiz

libro

tijeras

Name_____

Classroom Words

Answer each question with the correct Spanish word.

1. What do you sit on?
2. What do you erase with?
3. Where do you set your books?

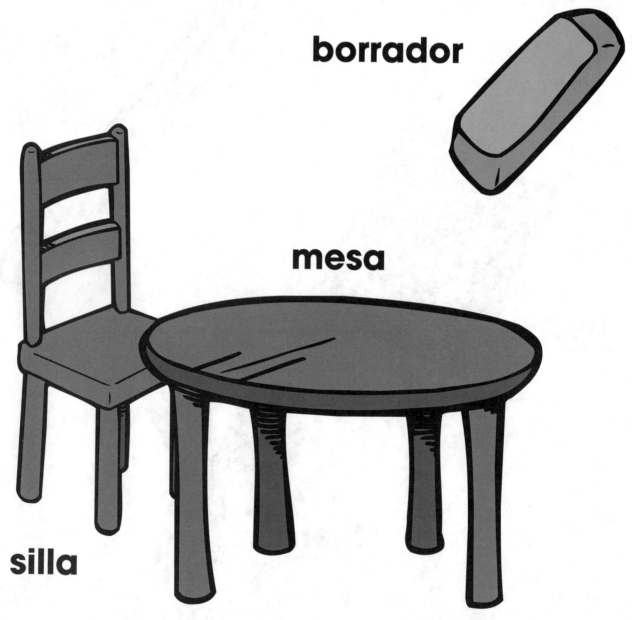

borrador

mesa

silla

Name_____

Classroom Words

Draw a picture of something in the classroom. Write the Spanish word. Color the picture.

```




```

_____

. . . .

_____

Community Words

Answer each question with the correct Spanish word.

1. Where do you go to play?
2. Where do you go to read?
3. Where do you go to learn?

biblioteca

escuela

parque

Name_____

Community Words

Answer each question with the correct Spanish word.

1. Where do you go to buy food?
2. Where do you go to learn about history?
3. Where do you live?

casa

tienda

museo

Name_____

Community Words

Draw a picture of something in your community. Write the Spanish word. Color the picture.

Name_____

Words Around the Home

The Spanish word for bedroom is **dormitorio**. Write the word on the line.

_____

. . . .

_____

The Spanish word for glass is **vaso**. Write the word on the line.

_____

. . . .

_____

The Spanish word for kitchen is **cocina**. Write the word on the line.

_____

. . . .

_____

The Spanish word for house is **casa**. Write the word on the line.

_____

. . . .

_____

Name_____

Words Around the Home

The Spanish word for living room is **sala**. Write the word on the line.

_____

. . . .

_____

The Spanish word for bathroom is **baño**. Write the word on the line.

_____

. . . .

_____

The Spanish word for towel is **toalla**. Write the word on the line.

_____

. . . .

_____

The Spanish word for bed is **cama**. Write the word on the line.

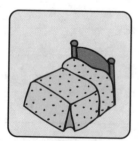

_____

. . . .

_____

Name_____

Words Around the Home

The Spanish word for stove is **estufa**. Write the word on the line.

The Spanish word for television is **televisión**. Write the word on the line.

The Spanish word for lamp is **lámpara**. Write the word on the line.

The Spanish word for telephone is **teléfono**. Write the word on the line.

Words Around the Home

Draw a line to match each English word to the same word in Spanish.

English	Spanish
bathroom	**casa**
towel	**estufa**
television	**dormitorio**
bedroom	**lámpara**
living room	**teléfono**
kitchen	**sala**
lamp	**vaso**
bed	**toalla**
telephone	**televisión**
stove	**baño**
glass	**cocina**
house	**cama**

Words Around the Home

Draw a picture of something around the home. Write the Spanish word. Color the picture.

Name_____

Family Words

Answer each question with the correct Spanish word.

1. What do you call your father?

2. What do you call your mother?

3. What do you call your brother?

madre

padre

hermano

Name_____

Family Words

Answer each question with the correct Spanish word.

1. What do you call your sister?

2. What do you call your grandmother?

3. What do you call your grandfather?

hermana

abuela

abuelo

Family Words

Write each family word. Then, color the pictures.

_____
....
_____

> **padre**

_____
....
_____

> **madre**

_____
....
_____

> **abuela**

_____
....
_____

> **abuelo**

_____
....
_____

> **hermano**

_____
....
_____

> **hermana**

Name_____

Family Words

Draw a picture of your family. Write the correct Spanish word next to each person in your picture.

padre	hermano	abuelo
madre	hermana	abuela

Name_____

The Human Body

Answer each question with the correct Spanish word.

1. What do you smell with?

2. What do you see with?

3. What do you hear with?

4. What do you chew with?

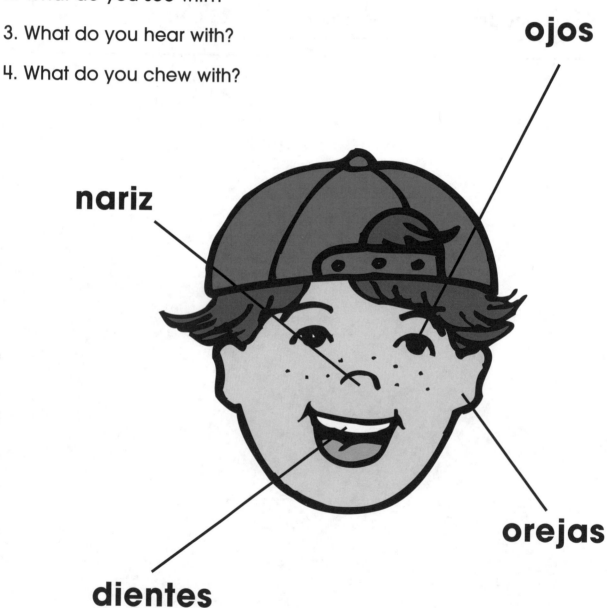

ojos

nariz

orejas

dientes

Name_____

The Human Body

Answer each question with the correct Spanish word.

1. What do you speak with?

2. What do you call your face?

3. What is on top of your head?

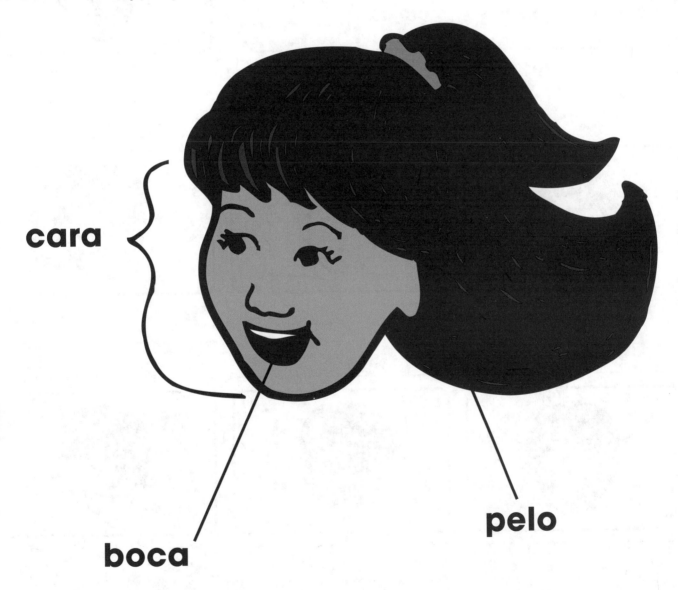

cara

boca

pelo

Name_____

The Human Body

Label each part of the face with a Spanish word from the Word Bank.

Word Bank

cara	ojos	boca	nariz
pelo	dientes	orejas	

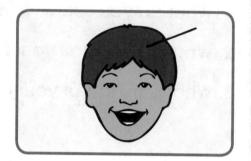

_____

....

_____

....

_____

....

_____

....

_____

....

_____

....

_____

....

Name_____

The Human Body

Write the Spanish word on the line that matches each face pictured.

happy

feliz

_____

....

sad

triste

_____

....

crying

llorando

_____

....

smiling

sonriendo

_____

....

angry

enojada

_____

....

thinking

pensando

_____

....

Name_____

The Human Body

Label each body part with the correct Spanish word.

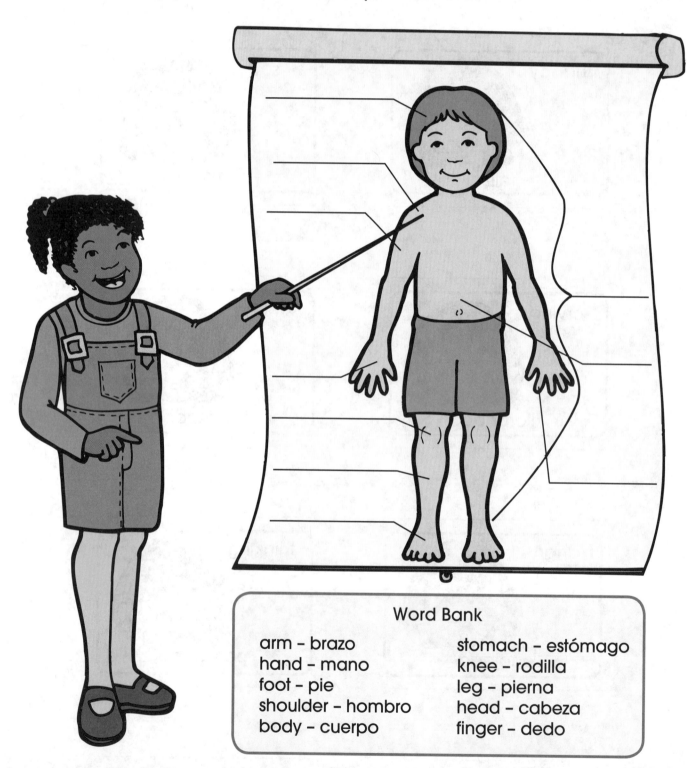

Word Bank

arm – brazo
hand – mano
foot – pie
shoulder – hombro
body – cuerpo

stomach – estómago
knee – rodilla
leg – pierna
head – cabeza
finger – dedo

Name_____

The Human Body

Draw a line to match each English word to the same word in Spanish.

body	**mano**
arm	**rodilla**
head	**cuerpo**
finger	**hombro**
hand	**estómago**
foot	**pie**
leg	**pierna**
knee	**cabeza**
shoulder	**dedo**
stomach	**brazo**

Name_____

Clothing Words

Answer each question with the correct Spanish word.

1. What do you wear on your head?

2. What do you wear with pants?

3. What does a girl wear?

gorra

vestido

camisa

Name_____

Clothing Words

Answer each question with the correct Spanish word.

1. What do you wear on your legs?

2. What do you wear on your feet to keep them warm?

3. What do you wear on your feet to go outside?

calcetines

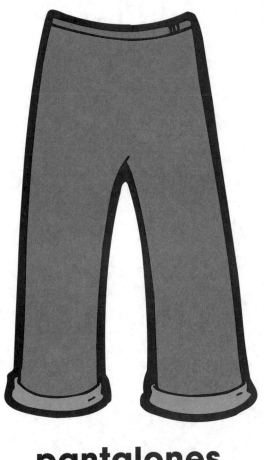

pantalones

zapatos

About You

Draw a picture of yourself from head to toe. Write the correct Spanish word next to each body part and the clothes you are wearing.

Name_____

Food Words

Answer each question with the correct Spanish word.

1. What do you eat that is meat?

2. What do you drink?

3. What do you eat that is made with vegetables?

leche

pollo

ensalada

Food Words

Answer each question with the correct Spanish word.

1. What do you drink with breakfast?

2. What is a vegetable that grows underground?

3. What do you use to make a sandwich?

4. What do you eat that is made from milk?

queso

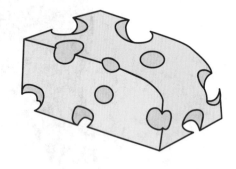

jugo

papa

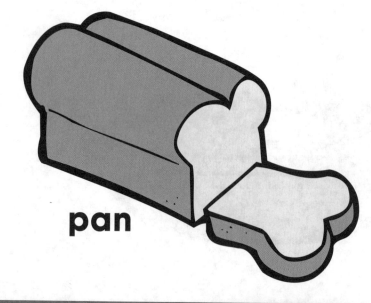

pan

Name_____

Food Words

Write each food word on the line. Then, color the pictures.

sopa

agua

naranja

carne

plátano

manzana

sándwich

Name_____

Food Words

Look at the graph. Then, answer the questions on the next page.

	manzana (apple)	queso (cheese)	sopa (soup)	pollo (chicken)
10				
9				
8			▓	
7			▓	
6	▓		▓	▓
5	▓		▓	▓
4	▓	▓	▓	▓
3	▓	▓	▓	▓
2	▓	▓	▓	▓
1	▓	▓	▓	▓

manzana
(apple)

queso
(cheese)

sopa
(soup)

pollo
(chicken)

Name_____

Food Words

_____
....

◆ How many people like manzanas best? _____
....

◆ How many people like sopa best? _____
....

◆ How many people like pollo best? _____
....

◆ How many people like queso best? _____
....

◆ Which food do most people like best? _____

◆ Which two foods do the same number of people like best?

_____
....

_____ and _____

◆ Which food do the fewest number of people like best?

_____
....

Food Words

Draw a picture of your favorite food. Write the Spanish word. Color the picture.

Animal Words

Answer each question with the correct Spanish word.

1. What lives on a farm?

2. What flies in the air?

3. What is a popular pet?

4. What catches flies for food?

5. What swims in a lake?

pájaro

perro

rana

pez

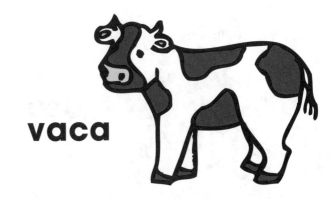

vaca

Name_____

Animal Words

Answer each question with the correct Spanish word.

1. What likes to play with yarn?

2. What lives near water?

3. What makes honey?

4. What sleeps in a cave?

5. What can you ride?

pato

abeja

gato

oso

caballo

Name_____

Animal Words

Write each animal word on the line. Then, color the pictures.

perro

gato

pájaro

pez

culebra

pato

Name_____

Animal Words

Count the animals in the window. Then, color one box for each animal on the graph.

6				
5				
4				
3				
2				
1				

pez (fish)	mono (monkey)	tortuga (turtle)	pájaro (bird)

Name_____

Animal Words

Draw a picture of your favorite animal. Write the Spanish word. Color the picture.

Name_____

Slow

The Spanish word for slow is **lento**. Trace the word.

Name_____

Fast

The Spanish word for fast is **rápido**. Trace the word.

Name_____

Hard

The Spanish word for hard is **duro**. Trace the word.

Name_____

Soft

The Spanish word for soft is **blando**. Trace the word.

Name_____

In

The Spanish word for in is **dentro**. Trace the word.

Name_____

Out

The Spanish word for out is **fuera**. Trace the word.

Name_____

Top

The Spanish word for top is **encima de**. Trace the word.

Name_____

Bottom

The Spanish word for bottom is **fondo**. Trace the word.

Name_____

Full

The Spanish word for full is **lleno**. Trace the word.

Name_____

Empty

The Spanish word for empty is **vacío**. Trace the word.

Name_____

Happy

The Spanish word for happy is **feliz**. Trace the word.

Name_____

Sad

The Spanish word for sad is **triste**. Trace the word.

triste

Name_____

Up

The Spanish word for up is **arriba**. Trace the word.

Name_____

Down

The Spanish word for down is **abajo**. Trace the word.

Name_____

Over

The Spanish word for over is **sobre**. Trace the word.

Name_____

Under

The Spanish word for under is **debajo de**. Trace the word.

Name_____

Hot

The Spanish word for hot is **caliente**. Trace the word.

Name_____

Hot

Draw a picture of your favorite thing to do when it's **hot**. Write the Spanish word for hot. Color the picture.

_____

....

_____

Cold

The Spanish word for cold is **frío**. Trace the word.

Name_____

Cold

Draw a picture of your favorite thing to do when it's **cold**. Write the Spanish word for cold. Color the picture.

_____

_____

Name_____

Left

The Spanish word for left is **izquierda**. Trace the word.

Name_____

Right

The Spanish word for right is **derecha**. Trace the word.

Name_____

Front

The Spanish word for front is **frente**. Trace the word.

Name_____

Back

The Spanish word for back is **atrás**. Trace the word.

Name_____

Above

The Spanish word for above is **arriba**. Trace the word.

Name_____

Below

The Spanish word for below is **debajo**. Trace the word.

Name_____

Zero

The Spanish word for zero is **cero**.

Color the number **0**.

Trace the number **0** in the second box below. Then, in the third box, write the number **0** on your own.

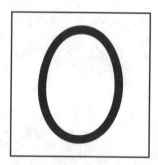 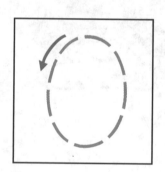 

Circle the box that shows **cero**.

Name_____

Zero

Trace the number. Trace the number word.

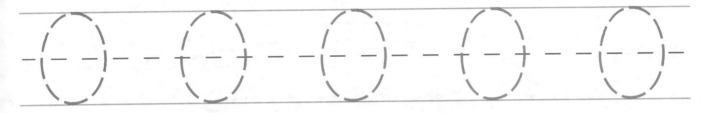

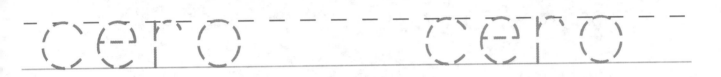

Now, practice writing the number and the number word on your own.

Zero

Color the fish with **cero** spots orange.

Name_____

One

The Spanish word for one is **uno**.

Color the number **1**. Color the one (**uno**) duck.

Trace the number **1** in the second box below. Then, in the third box, write the number **1** on your own.

 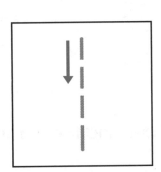 

Circle the box that shows **uno**.

Name_____

One

Trace the number. Trace the number word.

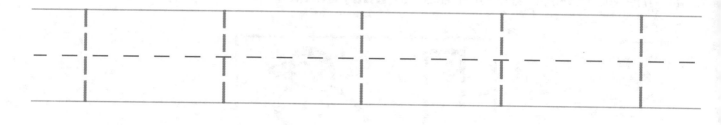

Now, practice writing the number and the number word on your own.

Name_____

One

Circle **I** picture in each box. Then, write **uno** on the line in each box.

Name_____

Two

The Spanish word for two is **dos**.
Color the number **2**. Color the two (**dos**) cats.

Trace the number **2** in the second box below. Then, in the third box, write the number **2** on your own.

Circle the box that shows **dos**.

Name_____

Two

Trace the number. Trace the number word.

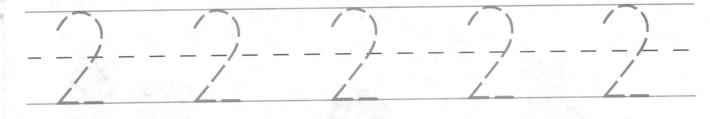

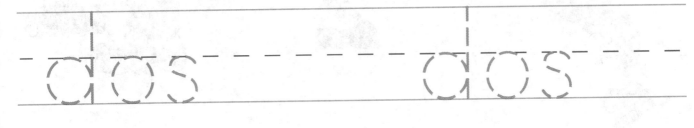

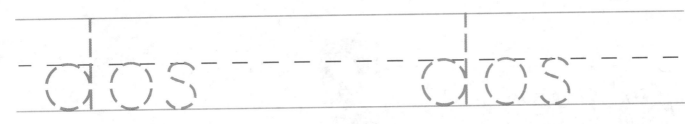

Now, practice writing the number and the number word on your own.

Name_____

Two

Draw a line to match each number **2** to a group of **dos** things.

2

2

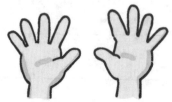

2

Name_____

Three

The Spanish word for three is **tres**.

Color the number **3**. Color the three (**tres**) dogs.

Trace the number **3** in the second box below. Then, in the third box, write the number **3** on your own.

Circle the box that shows **tres**.

Name_____

Three

Trace the number. Trace the number word.

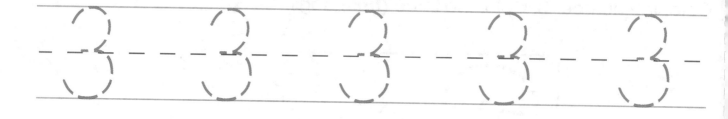

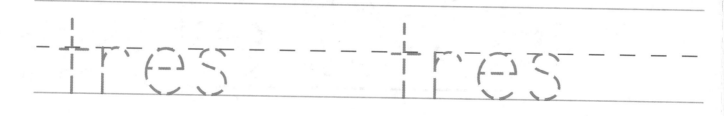

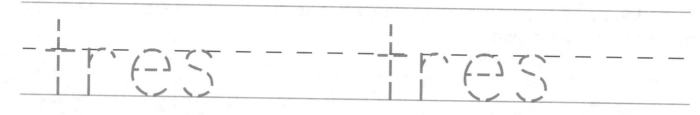

Now, practice writing the number and the number word on your own.

Name_____

Three

Color the spaces: **3** = verde, ••• = marrón, and **tres** = azul.

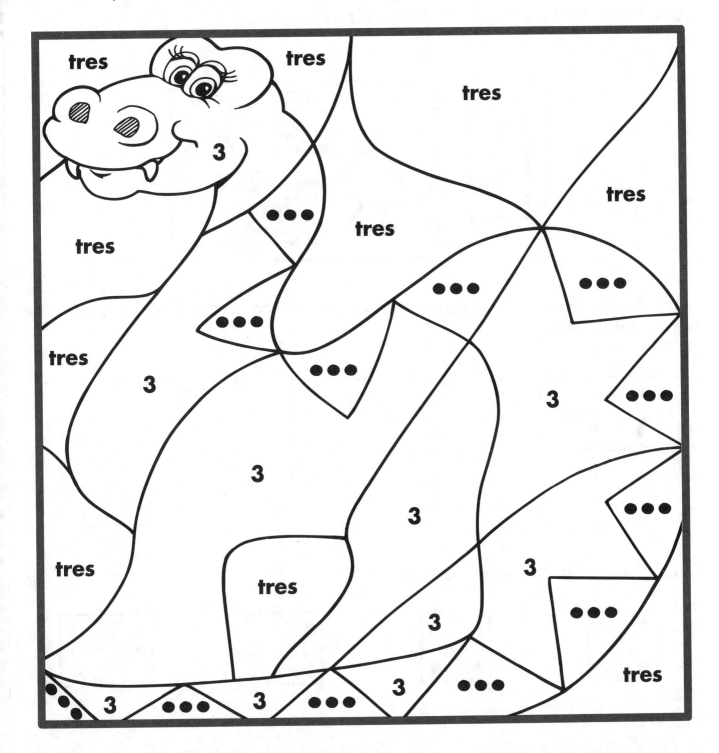

Name_____

Four

The Spanish word for four is **cuatro**.
Color the number **4**. Color the four **(cuatro)** animals.

Trace the number **4** in the second box below. Then, in the third box, write the number **4** on your own.

Circle the boxes that show **cuatro**.

   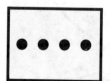

Name_____

Four

Trace the number. Trace the number word.

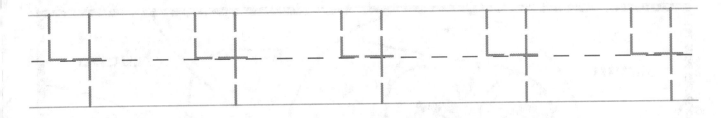

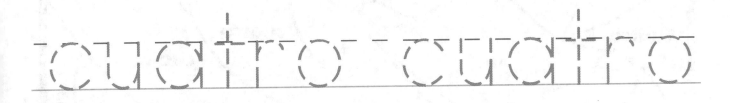

Now, practice writing the number and the number word on your own.

Name_____

Four

Color the spaces: **4** = amarillo, 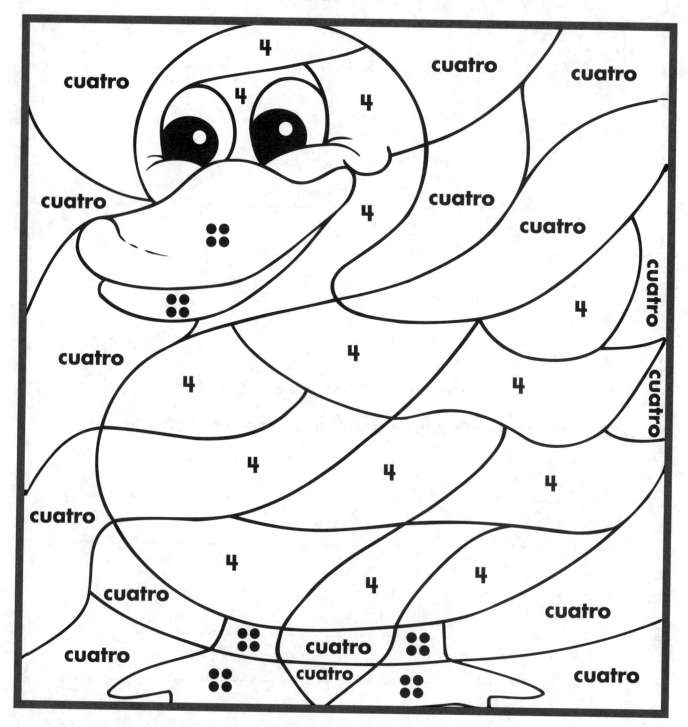 = naranja, and **cuatro** = azul.

Name_____

Five

The Spanish word for five is **cinco**.

Color the number **5**. Color the five (**cinco**) chicks.

Trace the number **5** in the second box below. Then, in the third box, write the number **5** on your own.

 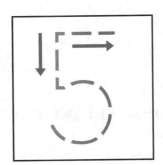 

Circle the boxes that show **cinco**.

  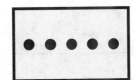

Name_____

Five

Trace the number. Trace the number word.

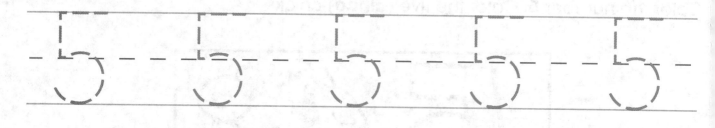

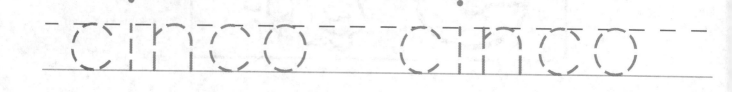

Now, practice writing the number and the number word on your own.

Name_____

Five

Count the shapes in each box. Draw more shapes so that each box has **5** shapes in it. Then, write **cinco** on the line in each box.

Name_____

Number Review 0-5

Trace the numbers.

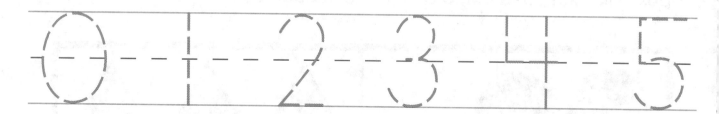

Practice writing the numbers on your own.

Write in the missing numbers.

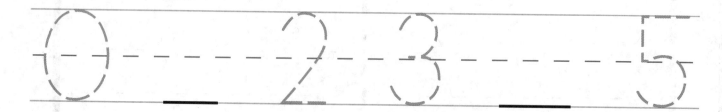

Name_____

Number Review 0-5

Trace the number words.

cero uno dos tres

cuatro cinco

Practice writing the number words on your own.

Write in the missing number words.

_____ uno _____ tres

cuatro _____

Name_____

Number Review 0–5

Color the spaces: **cero** = marrón, **uno** = rojo, **dos** = amarillo, **tres** = verde, **cuatro** = azul, and **cinco** = naranja.

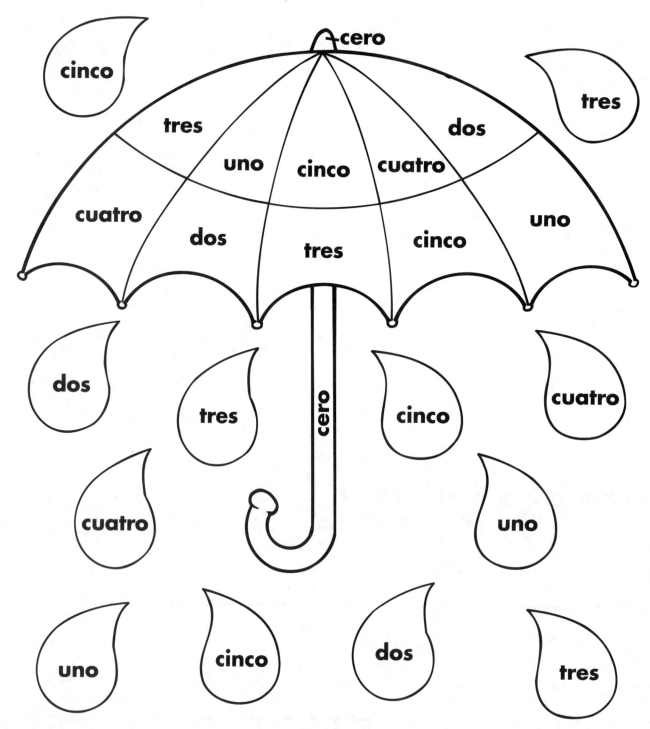

Name_____

Number Review 0–5

Count the fish. Trace the numbers and words. Draw a line to match the fish and the numbers.

 0 cero

 1 uno

 2 dos

 3 tres

 4 cuatro

 5 cinco

Name_____

Number Review 0–5

Count the things in each box. Then, write the correct number word on the line in each box.

Name_____

Six

The Spanish word for six is **seis**.

Color the number **6**. Color the six (**seis**) turtles.

Trace the number **6** in the second box below. Then, in the third box, write the number **6** on your own.

   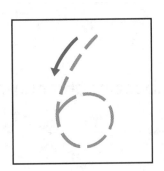

Circle the boxes that show **seis**.

Name_____

Six

Trace the number. Trace the number word.

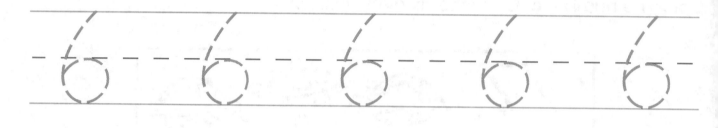

6   6   6   6   6

seis   seis

seis   seis

Now, practice writing the number and the number word on your own.

Name_____

Six

Circle **6** pictures in each box. Then, write **seis** on the line in each box.

Name_____

Seven

The Spanish word for seven is **siete**.
Color the number **7**. Color the seven (**siete**) butterflies.

Trace the number **7** in the second box below. Then, in the third box, write the number **7** on your own.

Circle the boxes that show **siete**.

Name_____

Seven

Trace the number. Trace the number word.

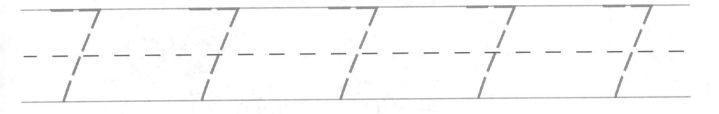

Now, practice writing the number and the number word on your own.

Name_____

Seven

Draw siete cookies in the cookie jar. Then, color the picture.

Name_____

Eight

The Spanish word for eight is **ocho**.
Color the number **8**. Color the eight (**ocho**) bees.

Trace the number **8** in the second box below. Then, in the third box, write the number **8** on your own.

 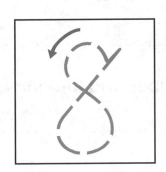

Circle the boxes that show **ocho**.

     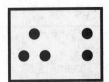

Name_____

Eight

Trace the number. Trace the number word.

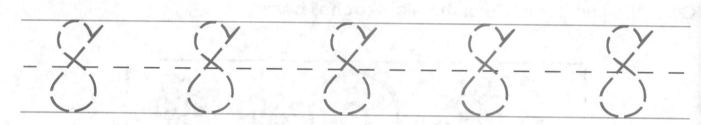

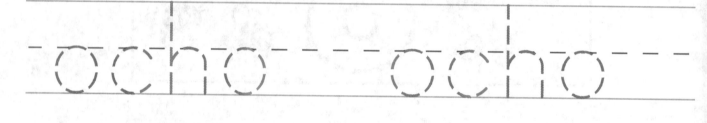

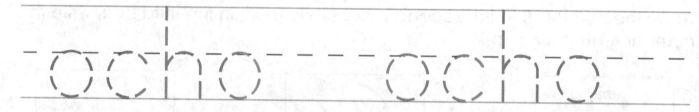

Now, practice writing the number and the number word on your own.

Name_____

Eight

Color the spaces: **8** = amarillo, = rojo, and **ocho** = verde.

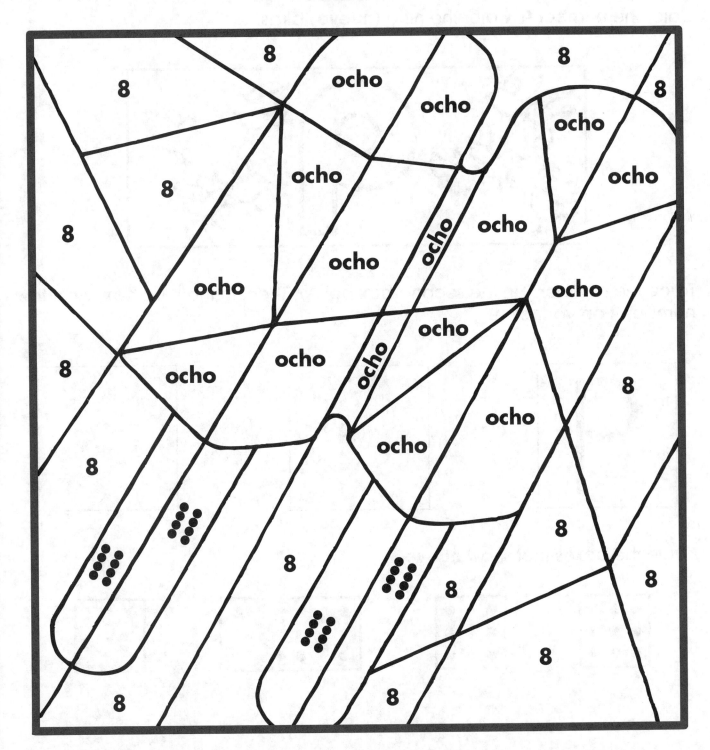

Name_____

Nine

The Spanish word for nine is **nueve**.
Color the number **9**. Color the nine (**nueve**) birds.

Trace the number **9** in the second box below. Then, in the third box, write the number **9** on your own.

 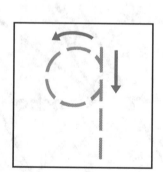

Circle the boxes that show **nueve**.

Name_____

Nine

Trace the number. Trace the number word.

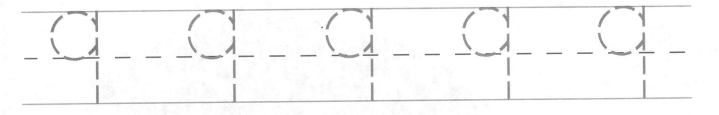

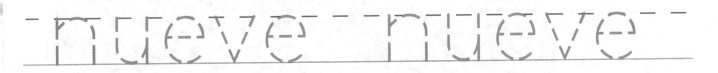

Now, practice writing the number and the number word on your own.

_____

- - - - - - - - - - - - - -

_____

- - - - - - - - - - - - - -

_____

Name_____

Nine

Draw **nueve** black dots on the ladybug's back.

Ten

The Spanish word for ten is **diez**.

Color the number **10**. Color the ten (**diez**) chipmunks.

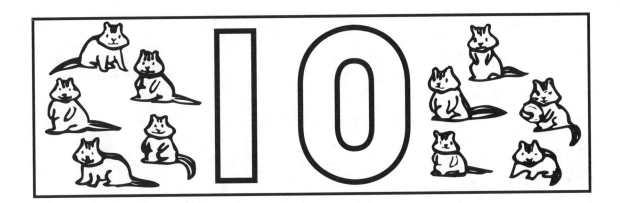

Trace the number **10** in the second box below. Then, in the third box, write the number **10** on your own.

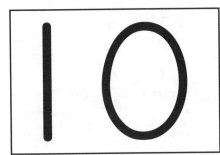 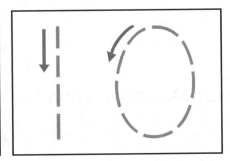 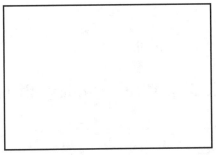

Circle the boxes that show **diez**.

  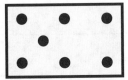

Name _____

Ten

Trace the number. Trace the number word.

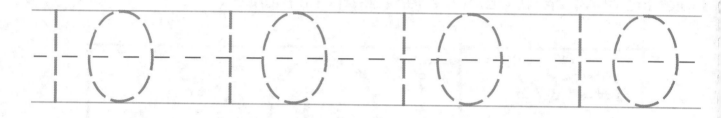

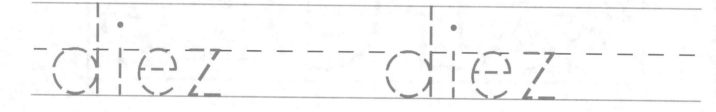

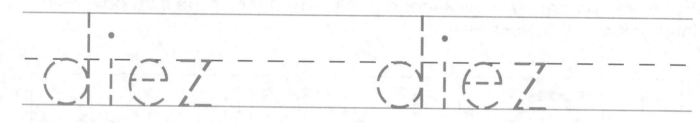

Now, practice writing the number and the number word on your own.

_____

— —

_____

— —

_____

Name_____

Ten

Color the spaces: **10** = blanco,  = amarillo, and **diez** = marrón.

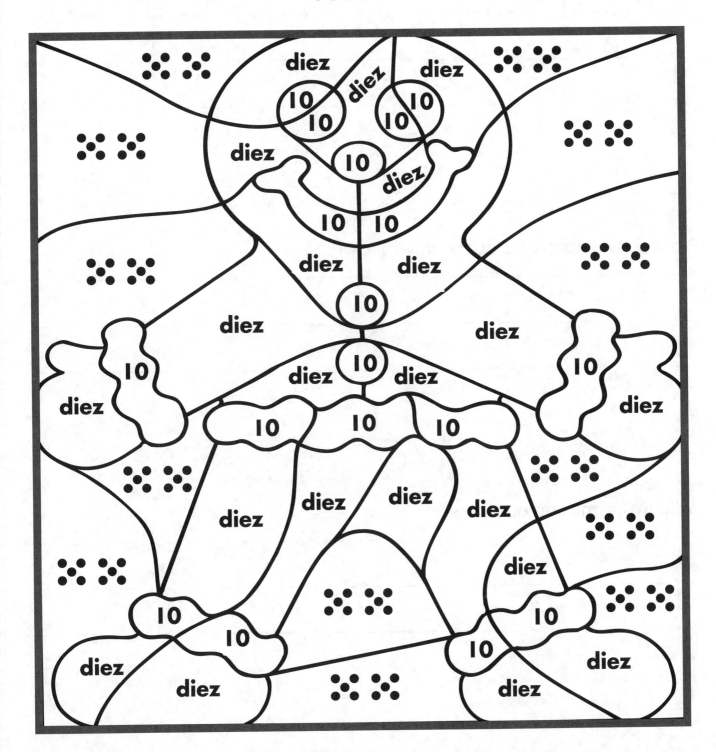

Name_____

Number Review 6-10

Trace the numbers.

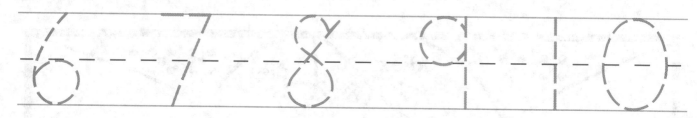

Practice writing the numbers on your own.

Write in the missing numbers.

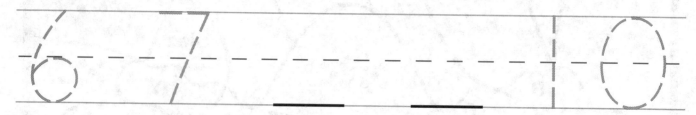

Name_____

Number Review 6-10

Trace the number words.

seis siete ocho

nueve diez

Practice writing the number words on your own.

Write in the missing number words.

seis _____ ocho

nueve _____

Name_____

Number Review 6-10

Color the spaces: **seis** = morado, **siete** = verde,
ocho = naranja, **nueve** = azul, and **diez** = amarillo.

Name_____

Number Review 6–10

Count the pictures. Trace the numbers and words. Draw a line to match the pictures and the numbers.

6 seis

7 siete

8 ocho

9 nueve

10 diez

Name_____

Number Review 6–10

Count the things in each box. Then, write the correct number word on the line in each box.

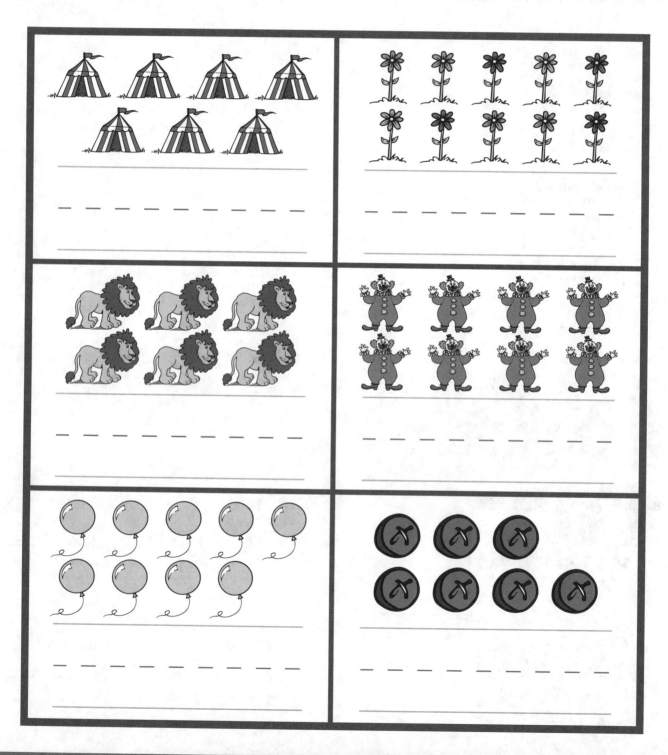

Name_____

Number Review 0-10

Trace the numbers.

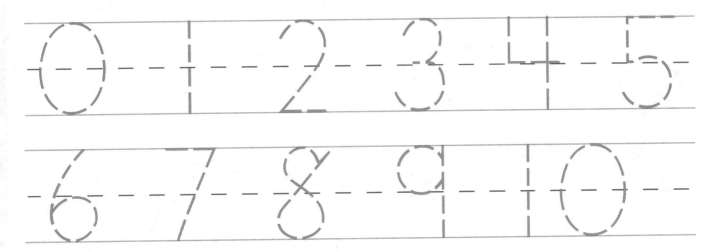

Write in the missing numbers.

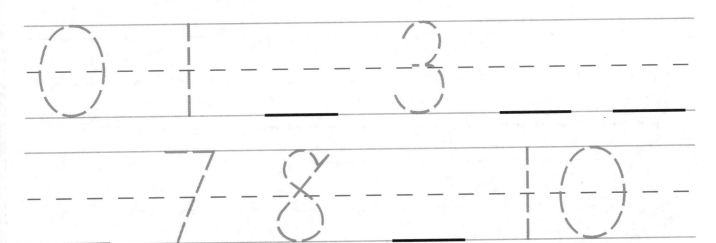

Name_____

Number Review 0-10

Trace the numbers again.

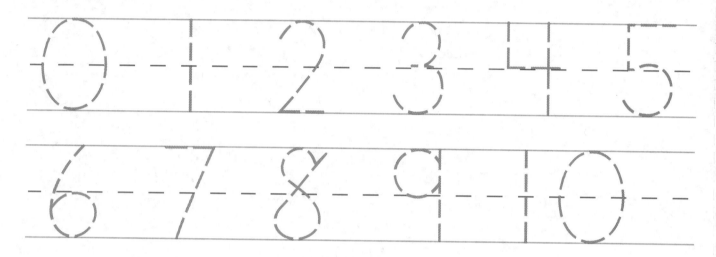

Write in the missing numbers.

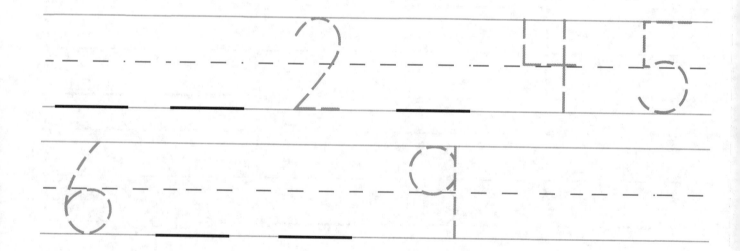

Name_____

Number Review 0-10

Trace the number words.

Name_____

Number Review 0–10

Write in the missing number words.

cero uno _____

tres cuatro _____

_____ seis _____

_____ _____ _____

nueve _____

Name_____

Number Review 0-10

Write in the missing number words.

_____ dos

_____

cinco _____

siete   ocho

_____ diez

Name_____

Number Review 0–10

Draw a line to match each creature to the correct number word.

tres

seis

uno

siete

dos

cinco

diez

cero

ocho

nueve

cuatro

Name_____

First

The Spanish word for first is **primero**.

Circle the picture that is **primero** in each row.

Name_____

Second

The Spanish word for second is **segundo**.
Circle the picture that is **segundo** in each row.

Name_____

Third

The Spanish word for third is **tercero**.

Circle the picture that is **tercero** in each row.

Name_____

Fourth

The Spanish word for fourth is **cuarto**.

Circle the picture that is **cuarto** in each row.

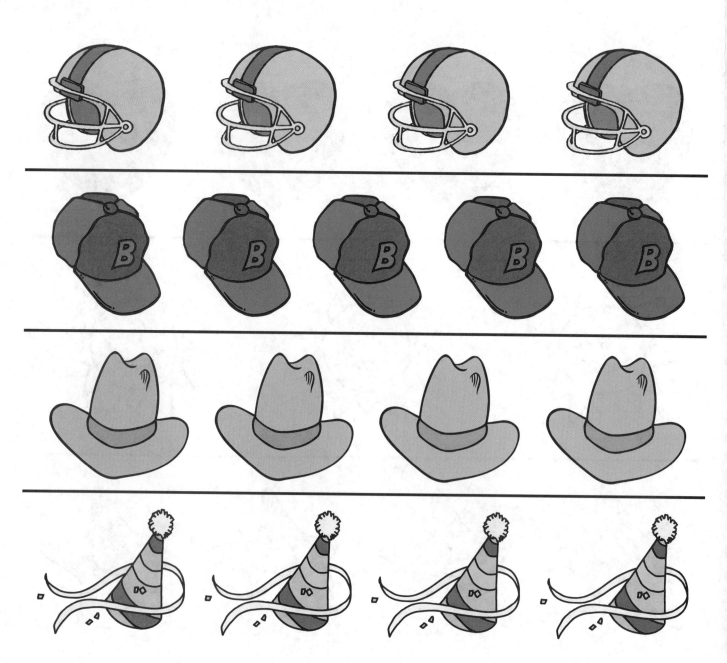

Name_____

Fifth

The Spanish word for fifth is **quinto**.

Circle the picture that is **quinto** in each row.

Name_____

Ordinal Numbers

Circle the person who is **tercero** in the line.
Draw a line under the person who is **segundo**.

Circle the person who is **primero** on the bench.
Draw a line under the person who is **quinto**.

Name_____

Ordinal Numbers

Circle the box that is **segundo**.
Draw a green line under the box that is **quinto**.

Draw red dots on the box that is **tercero**.
Draw a yellow bow on the box that is **cuarto**.

Ordinal Numbers

Draw an **X** on the tree that is **quinto**.
Draw a box around the tree that is **tercero**.

Draw a line under the tree that is **segundo**.
Circle the tree that is **primero**.

Name_____

Ordinal Numbers

Look at the pictures. What happened **primero**? What happened **segundo**?
What happened **tercero**?
Draw a line from the correct word to the picture.

primero

segundo

tercero

Ordinal Numbers

Write 1, 2, and 3 in the boxes to show what happens **primero**, **segundo**, and **tercero**. Then, draw a line from the correct word to the picture.

primero   segundo   tercero

Name_____

Patterns

The Spanish word for patterns is **pautas**.

Complete the shape **pautas**. At the end of the row, draw the shape that comes next. Then, color the shape.

cuadrado   **círculo**   **cuadrado**   **círculo** _____

cuadrado   **rectángulo**   **cuadrado**   **rectángulo** _____

rombo   **triángulo**   **rombo**   **triángulo** _____

Patterns

Complete the shape **pautas**. At the end of the row, draw the shape that comes next. Then, color the shape.

círculo　　**cuadrado**　　**círculo**　　**cuadrado**　　_____

rombo　　**círculo**　　**rombo**　　**círculo**　　_____

rectángulo　　**cuadrado**　　**rectángulo**　　**cuadrado**　　_____

Name_____

Patterns

Complete the **pautas**. Draw the picture that comes next in each row.

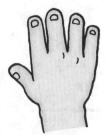 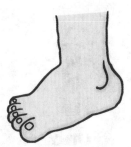 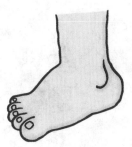 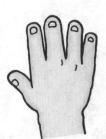 _____

mano **pie** **pie** **mano**

    _____

pelo **nariz** **pelo** **nariz**

     _____

feliz **feliz** **triste** **feliz** **feliz**

Name_____

Patterns

Complete the **pautas**. Write the number that comes next in each row.

1	2	1	2	1	_____
uno	dos	uno	dos	uno	

3	4	4	3	4	_____
tres	cuatro	cuatro	tres	cuatro	

8	7	8	7	8	_____
ocho	siete	ocho	siete	ocho	

Name_____

Patterns

Complete the **pautas**. Write the number that comes next in each row.

4 **9** **9** **9** **4** **9** _____
cuatro nueve nueve cuatro nueve

0 **7** **0** **7** **0** _____
cero siete cero siete cero

8 **2** **8** **2** **8** _____
ocho dos ocho dos ocho

Name_____

Same

The Spanish word for same is **igual**.

Look at the first picture in each row. Circle the other picture in the row that is **igual**.

Name_____

Different

The Spanish word for different is **diferente**.

Look at the first picture in each row. Circle the other picture in the row that is **diferente**.

Name_____

Same and Different

Look at the first picture in each row. Circle the other picture in the row that is **igual**. Draw a line under the picture that is **diferente**.

Name_____

Same and Different

Look at the first picture in each row. Circle the other picture in the row that is **igual**. Draw an **X** on the picture that is **diferente**.

Name_____

Big

The Spanish word for big is **grande**.
Color the picture in each row that is **grande**.

Name_____

Small

The Spanish word for small is **pequeño**.

Color the picture in each row that is **pequeño**.

Name_____

Big and Small

Color the shape in each box that is **grande**. Draw a line under the shape in each box that is **pequeño**.

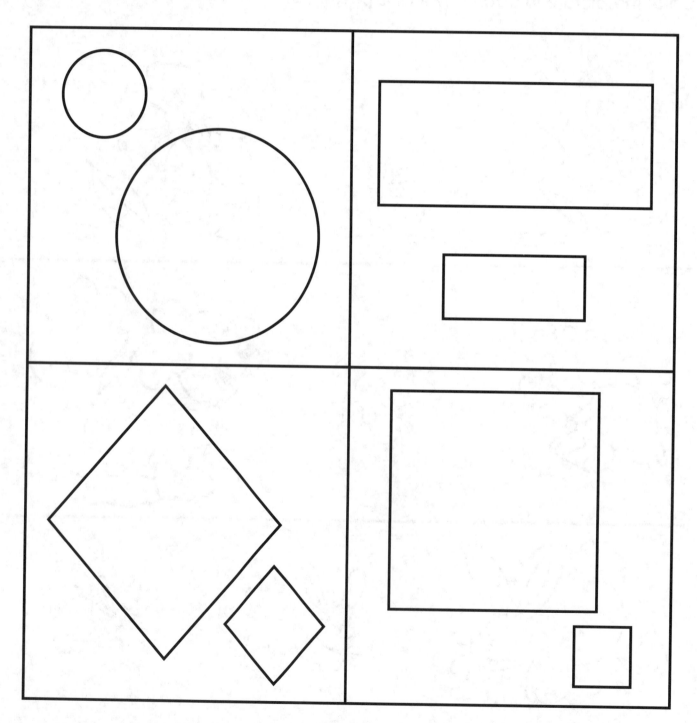

Name_____

Big and Small

Draw a line to match the shapes that are the same. Then, color each shape that is **grande** red. Color each shape that is **pequeño** green.

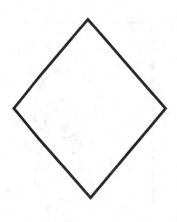

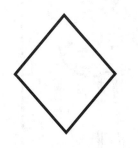
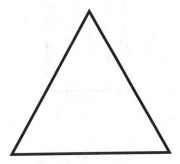
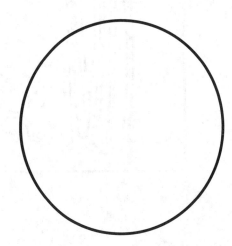

Short

The Spanish word for short is **bajo**.
Color the picture in each box that is **bajo**.

Name_____

Tall

The Spanish word for tall is **alto**.

Color the picture in each box that is **alto**.

Name_____

Short and Tall

Circle each person who is **bajo**. Draw a line under each person who is **alto**.

Name_____

Short and Tall

Draw a picture of you and your best friend. Write **bajo** or **alto** under each picture to describe yourselves.

Name_____

Long

The Spanish word for long is **largo**.
Color the picture in each row that is **largo**.

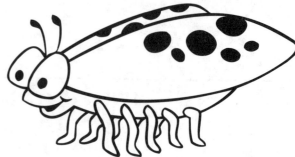

Name_____

Short

The Spanish word for short is **corto**.
Color the picture in each row that is **corto**.

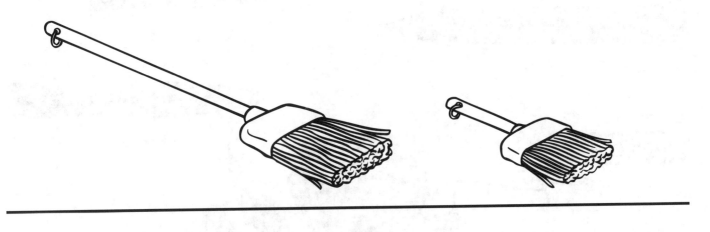

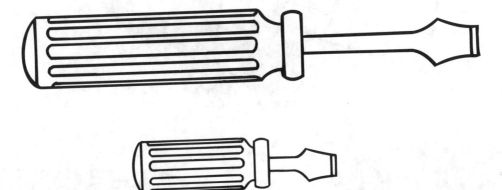

 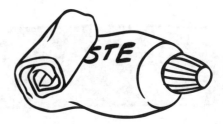

Name_____

Long and Short

Circle each picture that is **largo**. Draw a line under each picture that is **corto**.

Name_____

Long and Short

Draw something you play with that is long. Draw something else you play with that is short. Write **largo** or **corto** under each picture.

_____

_____

Name_____

More

The Spanish word for more is **más**.
Circle the group in each box that has **más**.

Name_____

Fewer

The Spanish word for fewer is **menos**.
Both children are playing with cars. Circle the child who has **menos**.

Name_____

More and Fewer

más 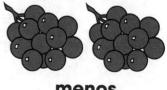 **menos**

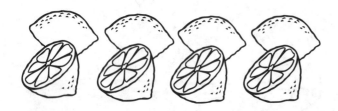 

Color the group that has **más**.

Color the group that has **menos**.

Name_____

Before

The Spanish word for before is **antes**.

Look at the pictures in the boxes. Circle the small picture below them that shows what happened **antes**.

After

The Spanish word for after is **después**.

Look at the pictures in the boxes. Circle the small picture below them that shows what happened **después**.

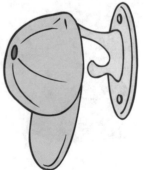

Name_____

First, Next, and Last

The Spanish word for first is **primero**.
Write **1** under the picture that happened **primero**.

The Spanish word for next is **luego**.
Write **2** under the picture that happened **luego**.

The Spanish word for last **último**.
Write **3** under the picture that happened **último**.

Name_____

First, Next, and Last

The Spanish word for first is **primero**.
Write **1** under the picture that happened **primero**.

The Spanish word for next is **luego**.
Write **2** under the picture that happened **luego**.

The Spanish word for last **último**.
Write **3** under the picture that happened **último**.

Name_____

Days of the Week

The Spanish word for day is **día**.

The Spanish word for week is **semana**.

There are seven days in one week. Each day of the week has its own name. Trace the lines to match each Spanish day of the week to the same day in English.

lunes   miércoles   viernes   domingo

martes   jueves   sábado

Monday	Tuesday	Wednesday	Thursday	Friday	Saturday	Sunday
		1	2	3	4	5
6	7	8	9	10	11	12
13	14	15	16	17	18	19
20	21	22	23	24	25	26
27	28	29	30			

Name_____

Days of the Week

Trace each Spanish day of the week. Then, practice writing each word on your own.

lunes   martes

miércoles   jueves

Name_____

Days of the Week

Trace each Spanish day of the week. Then, practice writing each word on your own.

Name_____

Days of the Week

Draw a line to match each Spanish day of the week to the same day in English.

miércoles

sábado

jueves

lunes

domingo

martes

viernes

Friday

Wednesday

Monday

Tuesday

Saturday

Sunday

Thursday

Name_____

Days of the Week

Choose your favorite day of the week. Write its name in Spanish on the line. Then, draw a picture of something you like to do on that day.

_____

_____

_____

Name_____

Months of the Year

The Spanish word for month is **mes**.
The Spanish word for year is **año**.

There are 12 months in one year. Each month of the year has its own name. Trace the lines to match each Spanish month of the year to the same month in English.

enero	- - - - - - - - - - - - -	**January**
febrero	- - - - - - - - - - - - -	**February**
marzo	- - - - - - - - - - - - -	**March**
abril	- - - - - - - - - - - - -	**April**

Months of the Year

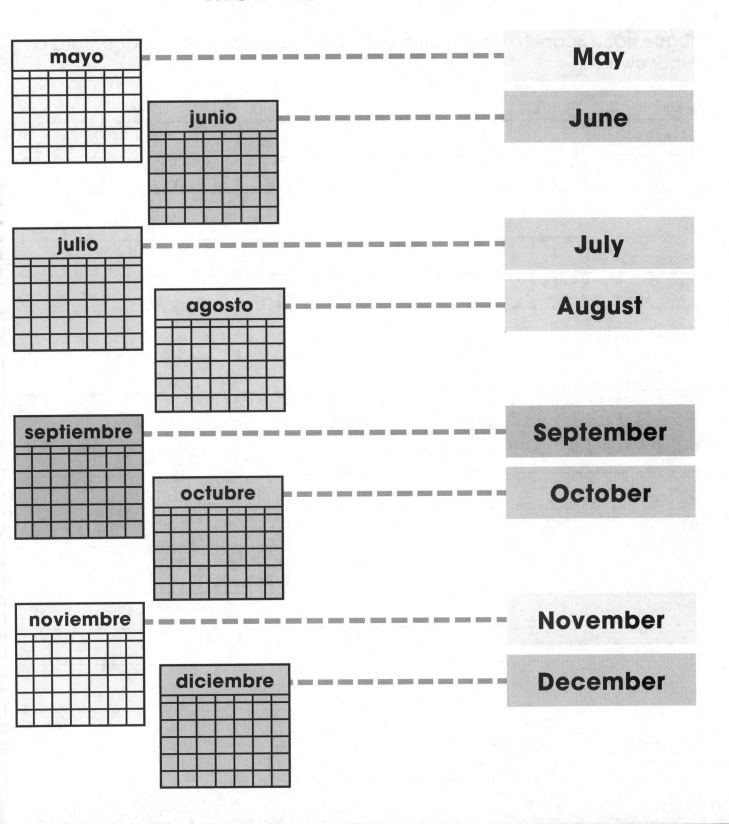

Name_____

Months of the Year

Trace each Spanish month of the year. Then, practice writing each word on your own.

enero febrero

marzo abril mayo

junio julio agosto

Name_____

Months of the Year

Trace each Spanish month of the year. Then, practice writing each word on your own.

septiembre

octubre noviembre

diciembre

Name_____

Months of the Year

For pages 354-357, use the word bank to write the Spanish month on the line below each English month. Then, in the box, draw a picture of something that happens in that month of the year.

Word Bank

agosto	septiembre	noviembre	mayo
junio	enero	octubre	febrero
marzo	julio	diciembre	abril

January

February

March

Name_____

Months of the Year

April	
May	
June	

Name_____

Months of the Year

July	
August	
September	

Name_____

Months of the Year

October	
November	
December	

Name_____

Winter

The Spanish word for winter is **invierno**.
Trace the word. Then, color the picture.

invierno

Name_____

Winter

These are things you wear in **invierno**.

bufanda

abrigo

mitón

Draw something else you wear in **invierno**.

Name_____

Winter

Draw something that you like to do in **invierno**.

Name_____

Spring

The Spanish word for spring is **primavera**.

Trace the word. Then, color the picture.

primavera

Name_____

Spring

These are things you see in **primavera**.

paraguas

lluvia

flor

Draw something else you see in **primavera**.

Name_____

Spring

Draw something that you like to do in **primavera**.

Name_____

Summer

The Spanish word for summer is **verano**.
Trace the word. Then, color the picture.

verano

Name_____

Summer

Draw something that you like to do in **verano**.

Name_____

Fall

The Spanish word for fall is **otoño**.
Trace the word. Then, color the picture.

otoño

Name_____

Fall

Draw something that you like to do in **otoño**.

Name_____

Weather Words

In the winter, it snows.
The Spanish word for snow is **nieve**.

Trace the word. Then, color the picture.

nieve

Name_____

Weather Words

In the spring, it rains.
The Spanish word for rain is **lluvia**.

Trace the word. Then, color the picture.

lluvia

Name_____

Weather Words

In the summer, the sun shines.
The Spanish word for sun is **sol**.

Trace the word. Then, color the picture.

S O l

Name_____

Weather Words

In the fall, the wind blows.
The Spanish word for wind is **viento**.

Trace the word. Then, color the picture.

viento

Name_____

Time

A clock can tell you what time it is.
The Spanish word for clock is **reloj**.

Trace the numbers and hands on the reloj. Then, color the **reloj**.

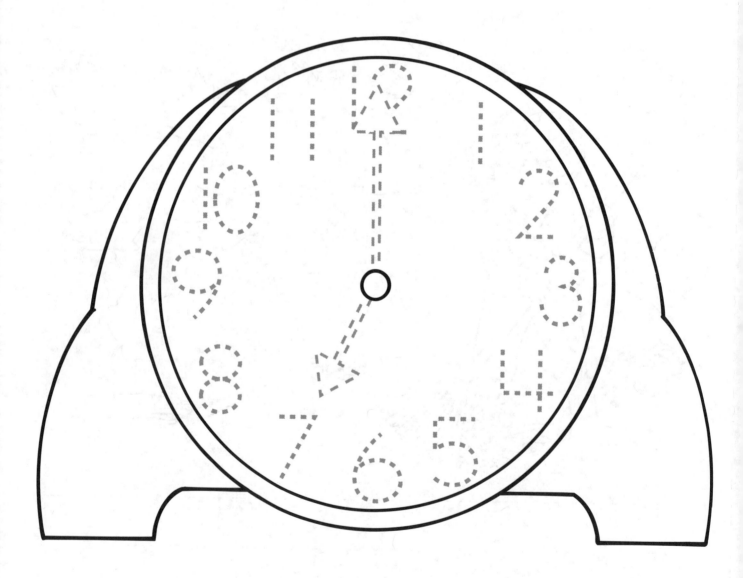

Time

Fill in the missing numbers on the **reloj**.

Time

The little hand on a **reloj** tells the hour. Draw the little hour hand on each clock.

8 o'clock

1 o'clock

7 o'clock

Time

Color the little hour hand red on each **reloj**. Then, write the correct number to complete each sentence.

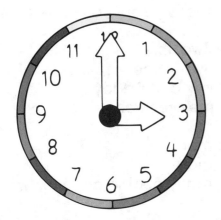

The **BIG HAND** is on _____.

The **little hand** is on _____.

It is _____ o'clock.

The **BIG HAND** is on _____.

The **little hand** is on _____.

It is _____ o'clock.

The **BIG HAND** is on _____.

The **little hand** is on _____.

It is _____ o'clock.

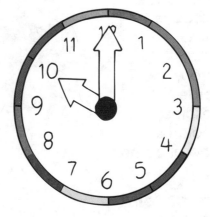

The **BIG HAND** is on _____.

The **little hand** is on _____.

It is _____ o'clock.

Songs and Rhymes

Uno, dos, tres
Uno, dos, tres.
Uno, dos, tres.
¿Cuántos son uno, dos, tres?

Uno, dos, tres.
Uno, dos, tres.
Mi mamá y mi papá
Y yo somos tres.

Uno más.
Uno más.
¿Cuántos son uno más?

Uno más.
Uno más.
Este es el niño.
Y con él somos cuatro.

One, Two, Three
One, two, three.
One, two, three.
How many people are one, two, three?

One, two, three.
One, two, three.
Mommy and Daddy
and me are three.

One more.
One more.
How many people are one, two, three?

One more.
One more.
This is the child
and with him are four.

¿Qué colores veo?
¡Veo, veo, veo!
¿Qué colores veo?
Ciruelas moradas,
tomates rojos,
maíz amarillo,
papas marrón,
lechuga verde.
¡Ay, que deliciosos!
¡Todos los colores
qué aprendo al comer!

What Colors Do I See?
I see, I see, I see!
What colors do I see?
Purple plums,
red tomatoes,
yellow corn,
brown potatoes,
green lettuce.
Oh, how delicious!
All the colors
that I learn to eat!

¡Cumpleaños feliz!
Cumpleaños feliz,
cumpleaños feliz,
muchas felicidades (nombre)
te deseamos a tí.

Happy Birthday
Happy birthday to you,
Happy birthday to you,
Happy birthday dear (name)
Happy birthday to you.

Songs and Rhymes

Colores

Este mi canto es
colores que puedo ver;
Los nombres aprender
asi lo voy hacer:
rojo, azul, verde, amarillo,
naranja, marrón y morado
negro, blanco son diferentes
¿Cuántos colores te he
mencionado?
—nueve—

Colors

This my song will be,
of colors that I may see;
The colors I need to know
I have to learn them so:
Red, blue, green, yellow,
orange, brown, and purple, too.
Black and white are not alike.
How many colors have I
mentioned?
—Nine—

La araña pequeñita

La araña pequeñita
Subió, subió y subió,
Vino la lluvia
y se la llevó.
Salió el sol.
y todo lo secó
Y la araña pequeñita
subió, subió y subió.

Itsy Bitsy Spider

Itsy bitsy spider
climbed up the spout.
Down came the rain
and washed the spider out.
Out came the sun
and dried up all the rain.
Itsy, bitsy spider,
climbed up the spout again.

Juan y Juana

Juan y Juana
subieron al monte
en busca de un cubo de agua;
Juan se cayó,
la crisma se rompío,
y Juana se despeño en la zanja.

Jack and Jill

Jack and Jill
went up the hill
to fetch a pail of water.
Jack fell down,
and broke his crown,
And Jill came tumbling after.

Treinta días trae septiembre

Treinta días trae septiembre
abril, junio y noviembre;
febrero tiene veintiocho,
y los demás treinta y uno.
Si año bisieto fuera
febrero traeriá veintinueve.

Thirty Days Hath September

Thirty days hath September,
April, June, and November,
February has twenty-eight,
and the rest have thirty-one.
If it were leap year,
February would have twenty-nine.

Songs and Rhymes

¿Qué hay de comer?

Hoy es lunes,
Hoy es lunes.
¿Qué hay de comer?
¿Qué hay de comer?
Lunes los ejotes.
Lunes los ejotes.
M-m-m, M-m-m.

Hoy es martes,
Hoy es martes.
¿Qué hay de comer?
¿Qué hay de comer?
Lunes los ejotes,
Martes los camotes.
M-m-m, M-m-m.

Hoy es miércoles,
Hoy es miércoles.
¿Qué hay de comer?
¿Qué hay de comer?
Martes los camotes,
Miércoles las fresas.
M-m-m, M-m-m.

Hoy es jueves,
Hoy es jueves.
¿Qué hay de comer?
¿Qué hay de comer?
Miércoles las fresas,
Jueves las cerezas.
M-m-m, M-m-m.

Hoy es viernes,
Hoy es viernes.
¿Qué hay de comer?
¿Qué hay de comer?
Jueves las cerezas,
Viernes el pescado.
M-m-m, M-m-m.

What's to Eat?

Today is Monday,
Today is Monday.
What's to eat?
What's to eat?
Monday, green beans.
Monday, green beans.
M-m-m, M-m-m.

Today is Tuesday,
Today is Tuesday.
What's to eat?
What's to eat?
Monday, green beans.
Tuesday, sweet potatoes.
M-m-m, M-m-m.

Today is Wednesday,
Today is Wednesday.
What's to eat?
What's to eat?
Tuesday, sweet potatoes.
Wednesday, strawberries.
M-m-m, M-m-m.

Today is Thursday,
Today is Thursday.
What's to eat?
What's to eat?
Wednesday, strawberries.
Thursday, cherries.
M-m-m, M-m-m.

Today is Friday.
Today is Friday.
What's to eat?
What's to eat?
Thursday, cherries.
Friday, fish.
M-m-m, M-m-m.

Songs and Rhymes

Hoy es sábado,
Hoy es sábado.
¿Qué hay de comer?
¿Qué hay de comer?
Viernes el pescado,
Sábado el helado.
M-m-m, M-m-m.

Hoy es domingo,
Hoy es domingo.
¿Qué hay de comer?
¿Qué hay de comer?
Algo hay de todo,
Y de este modo,
Lunes los ejotes,
Martes los camotes,
Miércoles las fresas,
Jueves las cerezas,
Viernes el pescado,
Sábado el helado.
¡Ay de mí! ¡Ay de mí!

Today is Saturday.
Today is Saturday.
What's to eat?
What's to eat?
Friday, fish.
Saturday, ice cream.
M-m-m, M-m-m.

Today is Sunday,
Today is Sunday.
What's to eat?
What's to eat?
Something of everything,
And in this order:
Monday, green beans,
Tuesday, sweet potatoes,
Wednesday, strawberries,
Thursday, cherries,
Friday, fish,
Saturday, ice cream.
Oh, my! Oh, my!

Los dedos
Esta es la mamá.
Este es el papá.
Este es el hermano mayor.
Esta es la hermana mayor.
Y éste es el bebé
y los queremos a todos.

Esta es la abuela.
Este es el abuelo.
Este es el tío alto.
Esta es la tía.
Estos son los primos
y queremos a todos.

The Fingers
This one is Mother,
This one is Father,
This one is the big brother,
This one is the big sister,
and this one is the baby,
and we love them all.

This one is Grandmother,
This one is Grandfather,
This one is the tall uncle,
This one is the aunt,
These are my cousins
and we love them all.

Songs and Rhymes

Buenos días
(Sung to: Frère Jacques)
Buenos días, buenos días.
¿Cómo está? ¿Cómo está?
Muy bien, gracias.
Muy bien, gracias.
¿Y usted? ¿Y usted?

Buenas tardes, buenas tardes.
¿Cómo está? ¿Cómo está?
Muy bien, gracias.
Muy bien, gracias.
¿Y usted? ¿Y usted?

Buenas noches, buenas noches.
¿Cómo está? ¿Cómo está?
Muy bien, gracias.
Muy bien, gracias.
¿Y usted? ¿Y usted?

Good Morning

Good morning, good morning.
How are you? How are you?
Very well, thank you.
Very well, thank you.
And you? And you?

Good afternoon, good afternoon.
How are you? How are you?
Very well, thank you.
Very well, thank you.
And you? And you?

Good evening, good evening.
How are you? How are you?
Very well, thank you.
Very well, thank you.
And you? And you?

Nombres de animales/Animal Names
(Sung to: The Farmer in the Dell)
El gato is the cat.
El gato is the cat.
Heigh-ho, the derry-o,
El gato is the cat.
                ——Sonya Kranwinkel
Additional verses:
El perro is the dog;
La gallina is the chicken;
El gallo is the rooster;
El caballo is the horse;
El pato is the duck;
La oveja is the sheep;
El cerdo is the pig.

Songs and Rhymes

Feliz Navidad/Merry Christmas

(Sung to: The Farmer in the Dell)
Feliz Navidad,

Feliz Navidad,

Feliz Navidad.

A Merry Christmas to you!
—Sue St. John

Cascabel

(Sung to: Jingle Bells)
Cascabel, cascabel,
Lindo cascabel.

Ringing notes of Christmastime,
Lindo cascabel.

Cascabel, cascabel,
Lindo cascabel.

Ringing notes of happiness,
Lindo cascabel.

—Aura Palacio

Jingle Bells

Jingle bells, jingle bells,
Pretty jingle bells.

Ringing notes of Christmastime,
Pretty jingle bells.

Jingle bells, jingle bells,
Pretty jingle bells.

Ringing notes of happiness,
Pretty jingle bells.

Contando en español/Counting in Spanish

(Sung to: Three Blind Mice)
One, two three; uno, dos, tres;

Four, five, six; cuatro, cinco, seis.

Counting in Spanish is fun to do.

You sing with me, and I'll sing with you.

Siete, ocho, nueve; seven, eight, nine.

Ten is diez. Ten is diez.
—Vicki Shannon

Songs and Rhymes

Lava, lava
(Sung to: Ten Little Indians)
Lava, lava tus manitas.
(Pretend to wash hands.)

Lava, lava tu carita.
(Pretend to wash face.)

Lava, lava tus dientitos,
(Pretend to brush teeth.)

Todas las mañanas.

Peina, peina, tu cabello.
(Pretend to comb hair.)

Ponte, ponte tu ropita.
(Pretend to put on clothes.)

Calza, calza tus zapatos,
(Pretend to put on shoes.)

Todas las mañanas.
          —New Eton School Staff

Wash, Wash

Wash, wash your little hands.

Wash, wash your little face.

Brush, brush your little teeth,

Every morning.

Comb, comb your hair.

Put on, put on your little clothes.

Put on, put on your shoes,

Every morning.

Me gustair/I Like to Ride
(Sung to: My Bonnie Lies Over the Ocean)
Me gusta ir en bus,
I like to ride the bus.

Me gusta montar mi triciclo,
I like to ride my trike.

Me gusta ir en carro,
I like to ride in the car.

Me gusta caminar,
I also like to walk.
          —Sonya Kranwinkel

Buenos días/Good Morning
(Sung to: Happy Birthday)
Buenos días a ti.

Buenos días a ti.

Buenos días, (name)

Buenos días a ti.
          —New Eton School Staff
English translation:
          Good morning to you.

Songs and Rhymes

Formas

(Sung to: The Bear Went Over the Mountain)
Un círculo hoy pintaremos

Con un dedito en el aire.

Un círculo hoy pintaremos,

Dando la vuelta así.
(Do actions as song indicates.)

Additional Verses:
Un triángulo hoy pintaremos;
Un rectángulo hoy pintaremos;
Un cuadrado hoy pintaremos.
—New Eton School Staff

El conejito/The Little Rabbit

(Sung to: Down by the Station)
Conejito,
Little bunny rabbit,
(Hold up two fingers.)

¿Dónde están sus huevos?
(Shrug shoulders)
Where are your eggs?

Conejito,
Easter is coming,

Hurry now
And hide your eggs.
(Put hands over eyes.)
—Sonya Kranwinkel

Shapes

Today we will draw a circle

In the air with a little finger.

Today we will draw a circle,

Going around like this.

Additional Verses:
Today we will draw a triangle;
Today we will draw a rectangle;
Today we will draw a square.

Los pollitos amarillos/ Pretty Yellow Chicks

(Sung to: Skip to My Lou)
Los pollitos amarillos,
Los pollitos amarillos,
Los pollitos amarillos,
Pretty yellow chicks.

Pío, pío, cheep, cheep, cheep;
Pío, pío, cheep, cheep, cheep;
Pío, pío, cheep, cheep, cheep;

Pío, pío, pío.
—Sonya Kranwinkel

abajo (a-BA-ho) down

abeja (a-BAY-ha) bee

abril (a-BREEL) April

abuela (a-BWAY-la) grandmother

abuelo (a-BWAY-lo) grandfather

agosto (a-GOS-to) August

agua (A-gwa) water

alto (AL-to) tall

amarillo (ama-REEL-yo) yellow

año (A-nyo) year

antes (AN-tes) before

arriba (a-RREE-ba) above

arroz (a-RROS) rice

atrás (a-TRAZ) back

azul (a-SUL) blue

bajo (BA-ho) below, short

baño (BA-nyo) bathroom

bebé (be-BAY) baby

biblioteca (bee-blee-o-TAY-ka) library

bicicleta (bee-see-KLAY-ta) bicycle

blanco (BLAN-ko) white

blando (BLAN-do) soft

boca (BO-ka) mouth

borrador (bo-rra-DOR) eraser

brazo (BRA-so) arm

caballo (ka-BYE-yo) horse

cabeza (ka-BAY-sa) head

calcetines (kal-say-TEE-nes) socks

caluroso (ka-lur-O-so) hot

cama (KA-ma) bed

camisa (ka-MEES-sa) shirt

cara (KA-ra) face

carne (KAR-nay) meat

casa (KA-sa) house

cero (SE-ro) zero

cinco (SEEN-ko) five

círculo (SEER-koo-lo) circle

cocina (ko-SEE-na) kitchen

conejo (ko-NAY-ho) rabbit

corto (KOR-to) short

cuadrado (kwa-DRA-do) square

cuarto (KWAR-to) fourth

cuatro (KWA-tro) four

cuerpo (KWAIR-po) body

culebra (koo-LAY-bra) snake

chica (CHEE-ca) girl child

chico (CHEE-co) boy child

debajo de (day-BA-ho day) under

dentro (DEN-tro) in

deportes (de-POR-tes) sports

derecha (de-RECH-a) right

después (des-PWES) after

día (DEE-a) day

diciembre (dee-see-EM-bray) December

Name_____

dientes (dee-EN-tes) teeeth

diez (dee-ES) ten

diferente (dee-fe-REN-te) different

dinero (dee-NAIR-o) money

domingo (do-MEEN-go) Sunday

dormitorio (dor-mee-TOR-ee-o) bedroom

dos (DOS) two

duro (DU-ro) hard

encima de (en-SEE-ma day) top

enero (e-NAIR-o) January

enojado (e-no-HA-do) angry

ensalada (en-sa-LA-da) salad

escuela (ess-KWAY-la) school

espejo (ess-PAY-ho) mirror

estómago (es-TOM-a-go) stomach

estrella (ess-TRAY-ya) star

estufa (es-TOO-fa) stove

febrero (fe-BRAIR-o) February

feliz (fe-LEES) happy

fiesta (fee-ESS-ta) party

flor (FLOR) flower

fondo (FON-do) bottom

frente (FREN-te) front

frío (FREE-o) cold

fuera (FWAIR-a) out

galleta (guy-YEH-ta) cookie

gato (GA-to) cat

globo (GLO-bo) balloon

gorra (GORR-a) cap

grande (GRAN-day) big

hermana (air-MAN-a) sister

hermano (air-MAN-o) brother

hombre (OM-bre) man

hombro (OM-bro) shoulder

huevo (WEH-bo) egg

igual (ee-GWAL) equal

insecto (in-SEKT-o) insect

invierno (een-bee-YAIR-no) winter

isla (EES-la) island

izquierda (ees-kee-YAIR-da) left

jabón (ha-BONE) soap

juego (HWAY-go) game

jueves (HWAY-bes) Thursday

jugo (HOO-go) juice

julio (HOO-lee-o) July

junio (HOO-nee-o) June

karate (ka-RA-te) karate

koala (ko-A-la) koala

lámpara (LAM-pa-ra) lamp

lápiz (LA-pees) pencil

largo (LAR-go) long

lento (LEN-to) slow

libro (LEE-bro) book

luna (LOO-na) moon

lunes (LOO-nes) Monday

llave (YA-be) key

lleno (YAY-no) full

llorando (yo-RAN-do) crying
lluvia (YU-bee-a) rain
madre (MA-dray) mother
mano (MA-no) hand
manzana (man-SA-na) apple
mariposa (mar-ee-POSS-a) butterfly
marrón (ma-RRON) brown
martes (MAR-tes) Tuesday
marzo (MAR-so) March
más (MAS) more
mayo (MY-o) May
menos (MAY-nos) less
mes (MASE) month
mesa (MAY-sa) table
miércoles (mee-YAIR-ko-les) Wednesday
mono (MO-no) monkey
morado (mo-RA-do) purple
museo (moo-SAY-o) museum
naranja (na-RAN-ha) orange
nariz (na-REES) nose
negro (NAY-gro) black
nido (NEE-do) nest
nieve (nee-YAY-bay) snow
noviembre (no-bee-YEM-bray) November
nube (NOO-bay) cloud
nueve (noo-AY-bay) nine
niña (NEE-nya) girl child
niño (NEE-nyo) boy child

océano (o-SAY-a-no) ocean
ocho (O-cho) eight
octubre (ok-TOO-bray) October
ojos (O-hos) eyes
orejas (o-RAY-has) ears
oso (O-so) bear
otoño (o-TO-nyo) fall
óvalo (O-ba-lo) oval
padre (PA-dray) father
pájaro (PA-ha-ro) bird
pan (PAN) bread
pantalones (pan-ta-LO-nes) pants
papa (PA-pa) potato
parque (PAR-kay) park
pato (PA-to) duck
pautas (POW-tas) patterns
pelo (PAY-lo) hair
pelota (pay-LO-ta) ball
pensando (pen-SAN-do) thinking
pequeño (pay-KAY-nyo) small
perro (PE-rro) dog
pez (PES) fish
pie (PEE-ay) foot
pierna (pee-YAIR-na) leg
plátano (PLA-ta-no) banana
pollo (PO-yo) chicken
primavera (pree-ma-BE-ra) spring
primero (pree-MAIR-ro) first

queso (KAY-so) cheese

quince (KEEN-say) fifteen

quinto (KEEN-to) fifth

rana (RA-na) frog

rápido (RA-pee-do) fast

rectángulo (rek-TAN-goo-lo) rectangle

regalo (re-GA-lo) present

reloj (re-LOH) clock

rodilla (ro-DEE-ya) knee

rojo (RO-ho) red

rombo (ROM-bo) rhombus

rosa (RO-sa) rose

sábado (SA-ba-do) Saturday

sala (SA-la) living room

sándwich (san-WEECH) sandwich

segundo (say-GOON-do) second

seis (SAYS) six

semana (se-MA-na) week

señora (se-NYO-ra) lady

septiembre (sep-tee-YEM-bray) September

siete (see-E-tay) seven

silla (SEE-ya) chair

sobre (SO-bray) over

sol (SOL) sun

sonriendo (son-ree-EN-do) smiling

sopa (SO-pa) soup

teléfono (te-LAIF-o-no) telephone

televisión (te-le-bee-see-OHN) television

tercero (tair-SAIR-o) third

tienda (tee-EN-da) store

tijeras (tee-HAIR-as) scissors

toalla (to-AY-a) towel

tortuga (tor-TOO-ga) turtle

tren (TREN) train

tres (TRAIS) three

triángulo (tree-AN-goo-lo) triangle

triste (TREES-te) sad

último (OOL-tee-mo) last

uno (OO-no) one

uvas (OO-bas) grapes

vaca (BA-ka) cow

vacío (ba-SEE-o) empty

vaso (BA-so) glass

ventana (ben-TA-na) window

verano (be-RA-no) summer

verde (BAIR-day) green

vestido (bes-TEE-do) dress

viento (bee-EN-to) wind

viernes (bee-YAIR-nes) Friday

watt (WATT) watt

xilófono (zee-LO-fo-no) xylophone

yema (YAY-ma) yolk

yogur (YO-gur) yogurt

zapatos (sa-PA-tos) shoes

zoológico (soo-o-LO-hee-ko) zoo

zorro (SO-rro) fox

Page 9

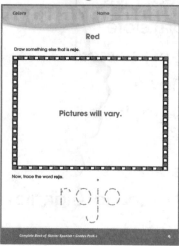

Page 10

Page 12

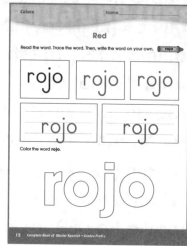

Page 13

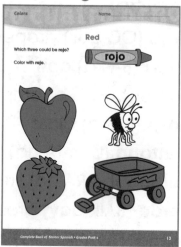

Page 14

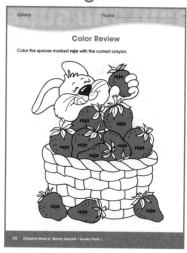

Page 16

Page 17

Page 19

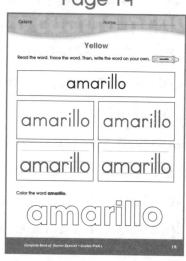

Answer Key

Page 20

Page 21
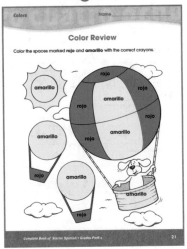

Page 23

Page 24

Page 26
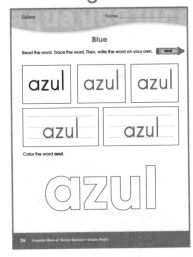

Page 27
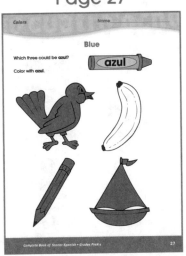

Page 28
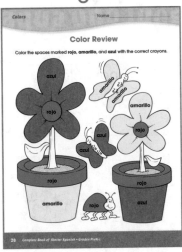

Page 30

Answer Key

Page 31

Green

Circle the picture that is **verde** in each row.

Page 33

Green

Read the word. Trace the word. Then, write the word on your own.

verde · verde · verde
verde · verde

Color the word **verde**.

verde

Page 34

Green

Which three could be **verde**?

Color with **verde**.

Page 35

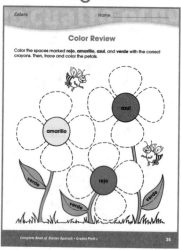

Color Review

Color the spaces marked **rojo**, **amarillo**, **azul**, and **verde** with the correct crayons. Then, trace and color the petals.

Page 37

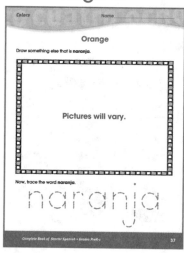

Orange

Draw something else that is **naranja**.

Pictures will vary.

Now, trace the word **naranja**.

naranja

Page 38

Orange

Circle the picture that is **naranja** in each row.

Page 40

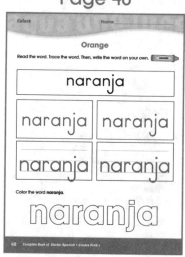

Orange

Read the word. Trace the word. Then, write the word on your own.

naranja
naranja · naranja
naranja · naranja

Color the word **naranja**.

naranja

Page 41

Orange

Which three could be **naranja**?

Color with **naranja**.

Answer Key

Page 42

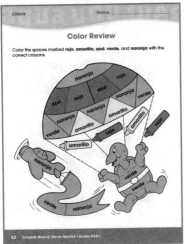

Page 44

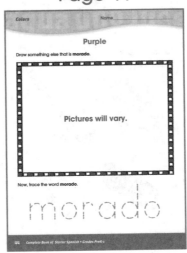

Page 45

Page 47

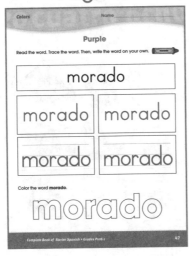

Page 48

Page 49

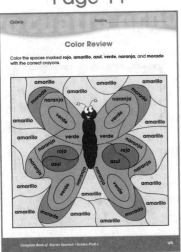

Page 51

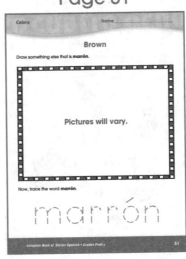

Page 52

Page 54

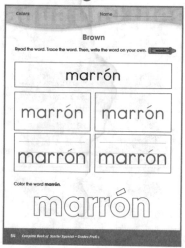

Page 55

Page 56

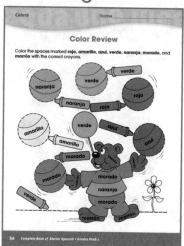

Page 58

Page 59

Page 61

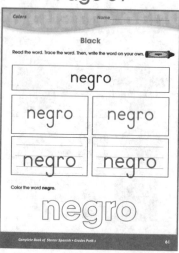

Page 63

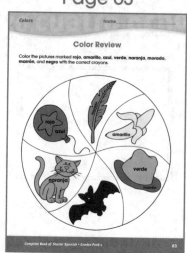

Page 65

Answer Key

Page 66

Page 67

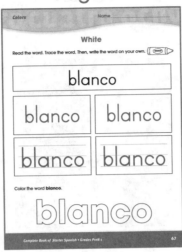

Page 69

Page 70

Page 71

Page 72

Page 73

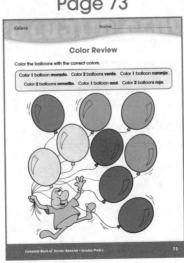

Page 74

Page 75

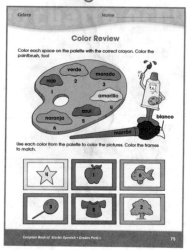

Page 79

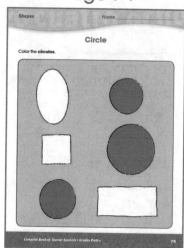

Page 80

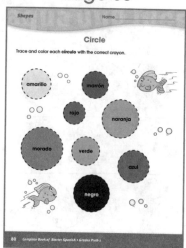

Page 81

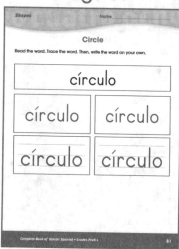

Page 86

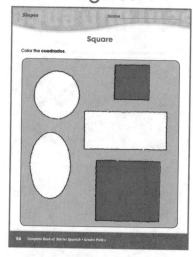

Page 87

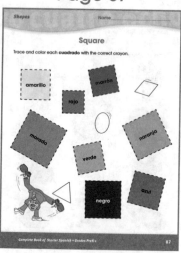

Page 88

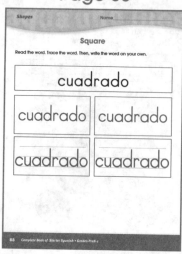

Page 93

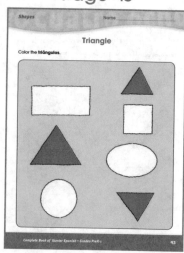

Page 94

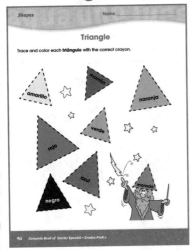

Page 95

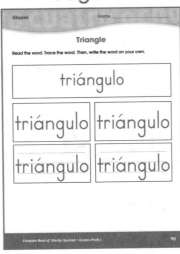

Page 100

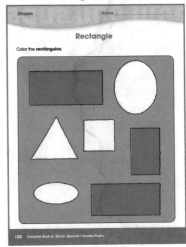

Page 101

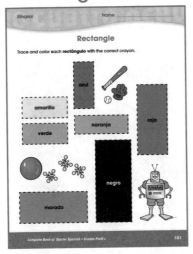

Page 102

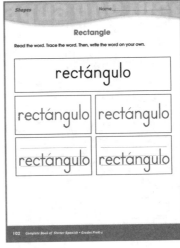

Page 107

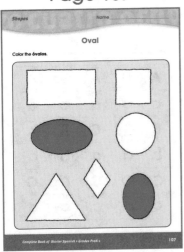

Page 108

Page 109

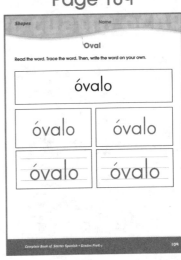

Answer Key

Page 114

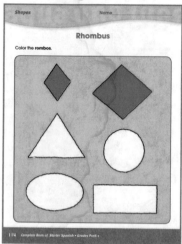

Page 115

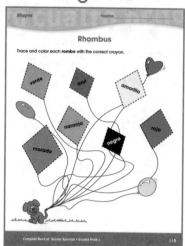

Page 116

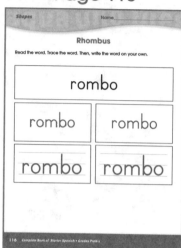

Page 118

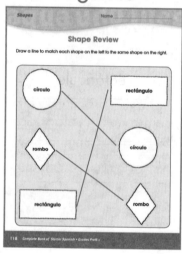

Page 119

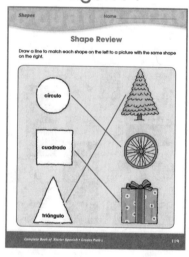

Page 120

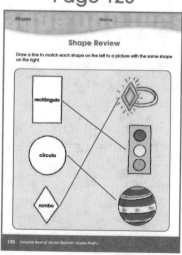

Page 121

Page 131

Page 140

Alphabet   Name_____

Letter Recognition

Circle the letters in each row that match the first letter.

D	B	G	(D)	B
d	b	(d)	a	(d)
E	H	F	(E)	(E)
e	(e)	a	b	(e)
F	E	(F)	E	A
f	t	(f)	l	o

Page 147

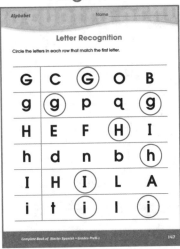

Alphabet   Name_____

Letter Recognition

Circle the letters in each row that match the first letter.

G	C	(G)	O	B
g	(g)	p	a	(g)
H	E	F	(H)	I
h	d	n	b	(h)
I	H	(I)	L	A
i	t	(i)	l	(i)

Page 156

Alphabet   Name_____

Letter Recognition

Circle the letters in each row that match the first letter.

J	(J)	U	L	(J)
j	g	(j)	q	i
K	N	F	H	(K)
k	l	h	(k)	b
L	J	I	(L)	U
l	t	(l)	l	i

Page 165

Alphabet   Name_____

Letter Recognition

Circle the letters in each row that match the first letter.

M	H	(M)	n	L
m	M	a	(m)	n
N	M	(N)	m	(N)
n	(n)	m	a	(n)
O	(O)	D	B	(O)
o	a	O	c	(o)

Page 174

Alphabet   Name_____

Letter Recognition

Circle the letters in each row that match the first letter.

P	D	(P)	O	b
p	(p)	d	q	b
Q	O	(Q)	G	(Q)
q	p	(q)	d	b
R	(R)	B	P	(R)
r	(r)	n	m	(r)

Page 181

Alphabet   Name_____

Letter Recognition

S	P	(S)	B	(S)
s	o	a	(s)	e
T	I	P	L	(T)
t	f	l	(t)	i
U	(U)	D	(U)	O
u	(u)	n	m	n

Page 186

Alphabet   Name_____

Letter Recognition

Circle the letters in each row that match the first letter.

V	W	(V)	A	N
v	w	x	(v)	y
W	V	M	A	(W)
w	(w)	v	x	m
X	Y	(X)	V	K
x	y	k	(x)	z

Page 191

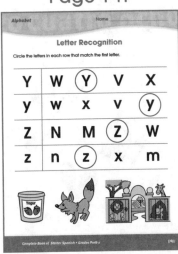

Alphabet   Name_____

Letter Recognition

Circle the letters in each row that match the first letter.

Y	W	(Y)	V	X
y	w	x	v	(y)
Z	N	M	(Z)	W
z	n	(z)	x	m

Answer Key

Page 192

Alphabet Name_____

Alphabet Review: Uppercase

Trace the uppercase letters. Write the missing uppercase letters.

A B C CH D E
F G H I J K
L LL M N Ñ O
P Q R S T U
V W X Y Z

Page 193

Alphabet   Name_____

Alphabet Review: Lowercase

Trace the lowercase letters. Write the missing lowercase letters.

a b c ch d e
f g h i j k
l ll m n ñ
p q r s t u
v w x y z

Page 194

Alphabet   Name_____

ABC Order

Put the Spanish words in **abc** order.

estrella	agua	isla
agua	estrella	isla

globo	vaso	queso
globo	queso	vaso

mariposa	zorro	nube
mariposa	nube	zorro

luna	huevo	dinero
dinero	huevo	luna

Page 195

Alphabet   Name_____

ABC Order

Put the Spanish words in **abc** order.

sopa	tren	regalo
regalo	sopa	tren

niño	uvas	libro
libro	niño	uvas

señora	chica	niña
chica	niña	señora

espejo	bebé	juego
bebé	espejo	juego

Page 196

Alphabet   Name_____

ABC Order

Put the Spanish words in **abc** order.

casa	bicicleta	abeja
abeja	bicicleta	casa

pelota	fiesta	insecto
fiesta	insecto	pelota

ventana	rosa	tijeras
rosa	tijeras	ventana

yema	pez	chico
chico	pez	yema

Page 197

Classroom Objects   Name_____

Classroom Words

Answer each question with the correct Spanish word.

1. libro
2. tijeras
3. lápiz

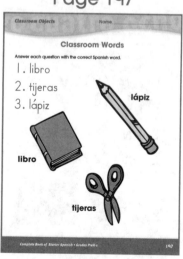

lápiz

libro

tijeras

Page 198

Classroom Objects   Name_____

Classroom Words

Answer each question with the correct Spanish word.

1. silla
2. borrador
3. mesa

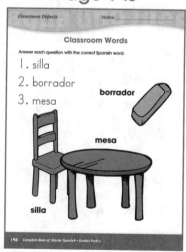

borrador

mesa

silla

Page 199

Classroom Objects   Name_____

Classroom Words

Draw a picture of something in the classroom. Write the Spanish word. Color the picture.

Pictures will vary.

Answer Key

Page 200

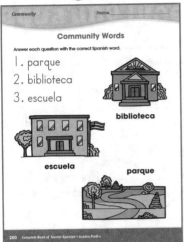

Community · Name_____

Community Words

Answer each question with the correct Spanish word.

1. parque
2. biblioteca
3. escuela

biblioteca

escuela

parque

Page 201

Community · Name_____

Community Words

Answer each question with the correct Spanish word.

1. tienda
2. museo
3. casa

tienda

casa

museo

Page 202

Community · Name_____

Community Words

Draw a picture of something in your community. Write the Spanish word. Color the picture.

Pictures will vary.

Page 203

Community · Name_____

Words Around the Home

The Spanish word for bedroom is **dormitorio**. Write the word on the line.

dormitorio

The Spanish word for glass is **vaso**. Write the word on the line.

vaso

The Spanish word for kitchen is **cocina**. Write the word on the line.

cocina

The Spanish word for house is **casa**. Write the word on the line.

casa

Page 204

Community · Name_____

Words Around the Home

The Spanish word for living room is **sala**. Write the word on the line.

sala

The Spanish word for bathroom is **baño**. Write the word on the line.

baño

The Spanish word for towel is **toalla**. Write the word on the line.

toalla

The Spanish word for bed is **cama**. Write the word on the line.

cama

Page 205

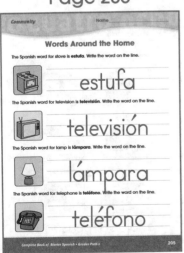

Community · Name_____

Words Around the Home

The Spanish word for stove is **estufa**. Write the word on the line.

estufa

The Spanish word for television is **televisión**. Write the word on the line.

televisión

The Spanish word for lamp is **lámpara**. Write the word on the line.

lámpara

The Spanish word for telephone is **teléfono**. Write the word on the line.

teléfono

Page 206

Community · Name_____

Words Around the Home

Draw a line to match each English word to the same word in Spanish.

bathroom — baño
towel — toalla
television — televisión
bedroom — dormitorio
living room — sala
kitchen — cocina
lamp — lámpara
bed — cama
telephone — teléfono
stove — estufa
glass — vaso
house — casa

Page 207

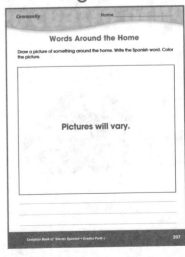

Community · Name_____

Words Around the Home

Draw a picture of something around the home. Write the Spanish word. Color the picture.

Pictures will vary.

Page 208

Page 209

Page 210

Page 211

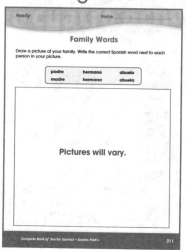

Page 212

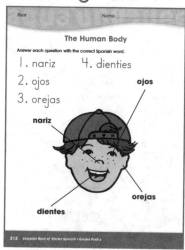

Page 213

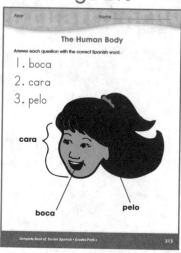

Page 214

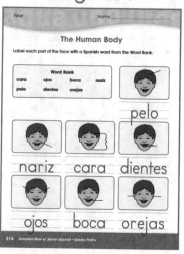

Page 215

Page 216

The Human Body

Label each body part with the correct Spanish word.

cabeza
hombro
brazo
cuerpo
mano
estómago
rodilla
pierna
dedo
pie

Word Bank
arm – brazo   stomach – estómago
hand – mano   knee – rodilla
foot – pie   leg – pierna
shoulder – hombro   head – cabeza
body – cuerpo   finger – dedo

Page 217

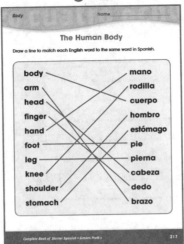

The Human Body

Draw a line to match each English word to the same word in Spanish.

body	mano
arm	rodilla
head	cuerpo
finger	hombro
hand	estómago
foot	pie
leg	pierna
knee	cabeza
shoulder	dedo
stomach	brazo

Page 218

Clothing Words

Answer each question with the correct Spanish word.

1. gorra
2. camisa
3. vestido

vestido
gorra
camisa

Page 219

Clothing Words

Answer each question with the correct Spanish word.

1. pantalones
2. calcetines
3. zapatos

calcetines
zapatos
pantalones

Page 220

About You

Draw a picture of yourself from head to toe. Write the correct Spanish word next to each body part and the clothes you are wearing.

Pictures will vary.

Page 221

Food Words

Answer each question with the correct Spanish word.

1. pollo   3. ensalada
2. leche

leche
pollo
ensalada

Page 222

Food Words

Answer each question with the correct Spanish word.

1. jugo   3. pan
2. papa   4. queso

queso
jugo
papa
pan

Page 223

Food Words

Write each food word on the line. Then, color the pictures.

sopa
agua
naranja
carne
Colors will vary.
plátano
manzana
plátano
sándwich
manzana
sándwich

Answer Key

Page 224

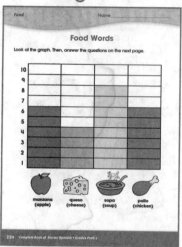

Page 225

Page 226

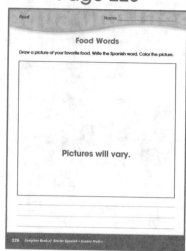

Page 227

Page 228

Page 229

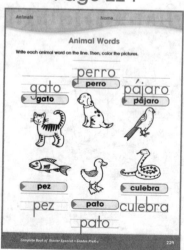

Page 230

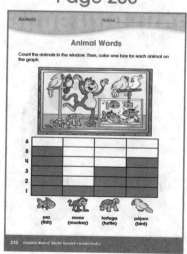

Page 231

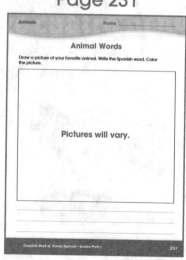

Answer Key

Page 249

Page 251

Page 258

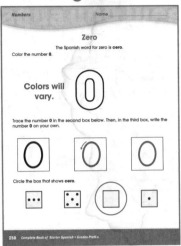

Page 260

Page 261

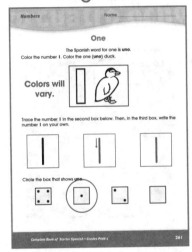

Page 263

Page 264

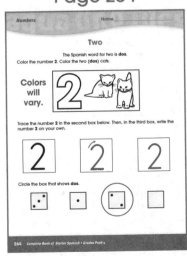

Page 266

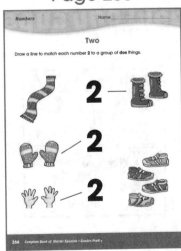

Page 267

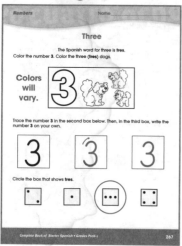

Page 269

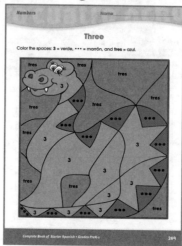

Page 270

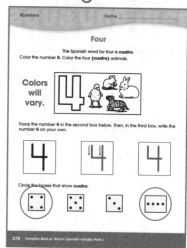

Page 272

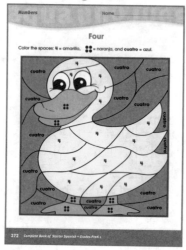

Page 273

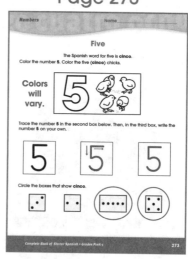

Page 275

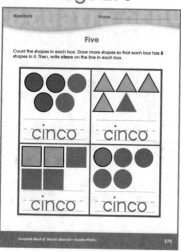

Page 276

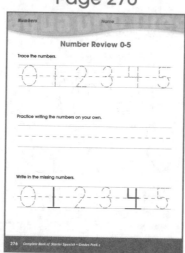

Page 277

Answer Key

Page 278

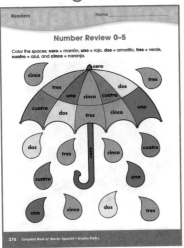

Page 279

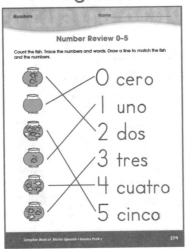

Page 280

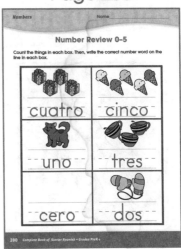

Page 281

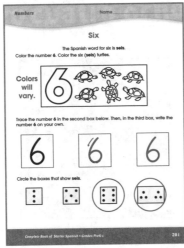

Page 283

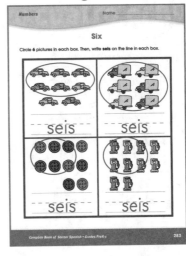

Page 284

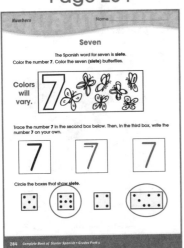

Page 286

Page 287

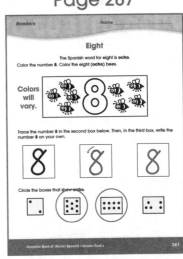

Page 289

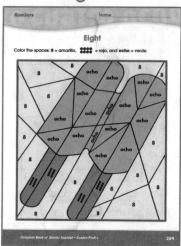

Page 290

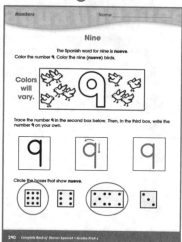

Page 292

Page 293

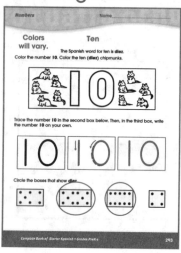

Page 295

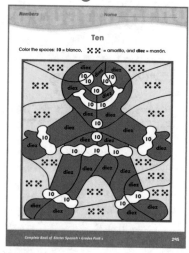

Page 296

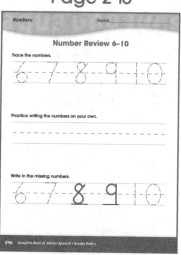

Page 297

Page 298

Page 299

Page 300

Page 301

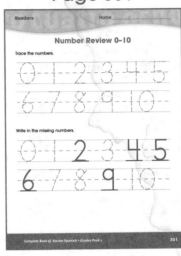

Page 302

Page 304

Page 305

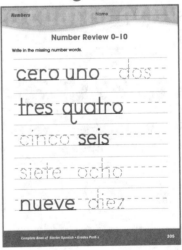

Page 306

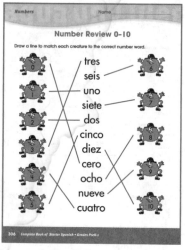

Page 307

Page 308

Page 309

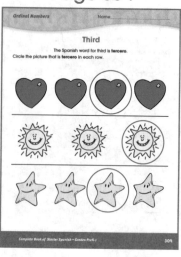

Page 310

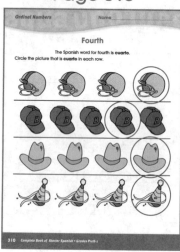

Page 311

Answer Key

Page 312

Page 313

Page 314

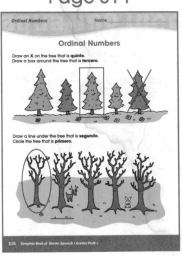

Page 315

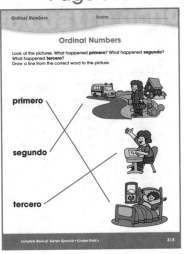

Page 316

Page 317

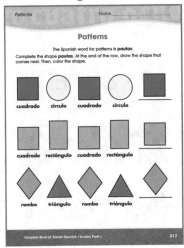

Answer Key

Page 318

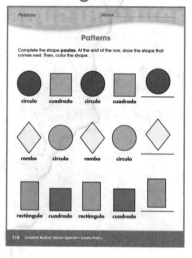

Page 319

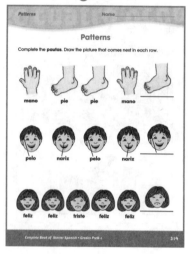

Page 320

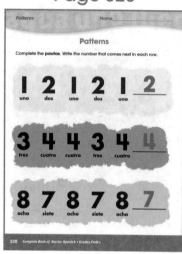

Page 321

Page 322

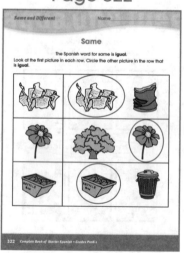

Page 323

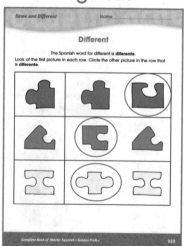

Answer Key

Page 324

Page 325

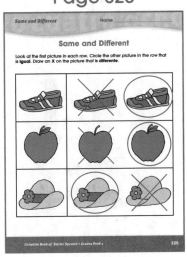

Page 326

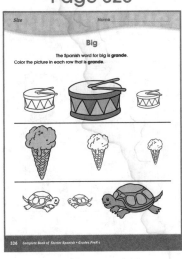

Page 327

Page 328

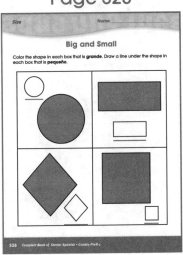

Page 329

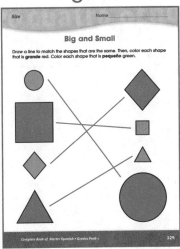

Page 330

Page 331

Page 332

Page 333

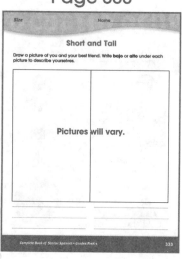

Page 334

Page 335

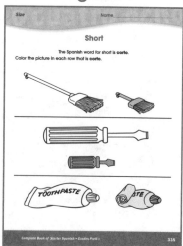

Answer Key

Page 336

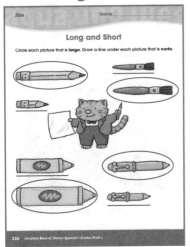

Page 337

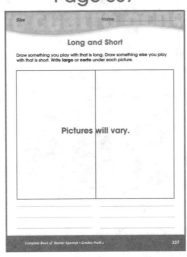

Page 338

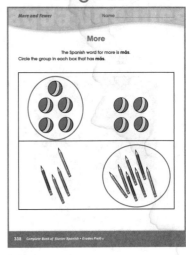

Page 339

Page 340

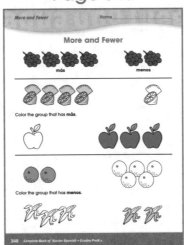

Page 341

Page 342

Sequence Name

After

The Spanish word for after is **después**.
Look at the pictures in the boxes. Circle the small picture below them that shows what happened **después**.

342 Complete Book of Starter Spanish • Grades PreK-1

Page 343

Sequence Name

First, Next, and Last

The Spanish word for first is **primero**.
Write **1** under the picture that happened **primero**.

The Spanish word for next is **luego**.
Write **2** under the picture that happened **luego**.

The Spanish word for last is **último**.
Write **3** under the picture that happened **último**.

3   1   2

Complete Book of Starter Spanish • Grades PreK-1 343

Page 344

Sequence Name

First, Next, and Last

The Spanish word for first is **primero**.
Write **1** under the picture that happened **primero**.

The Spanish word for next is **luego**.
Write **2** under the picture that happened **luego**.

The Spanish word for last is **último**.
Write **3** under the picture that happened **último**.

2   3   1

344 Complete Book of Starter Spanish • Grades PreK-1

Page 348

Days of the Week Name

Days of the Week

Draw a line to match each Spanish day of the week to the same day in English.

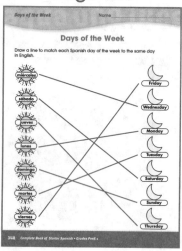

348 Complete Book of Starter Spanish • Grades PreK-1

Page 349

Days of the Week Name

Days of the Week

Choose your favorite day of the week. Write its name in Spanish on the line. Then, draw a picture of something you like to do on that day.

Pictures will vary.

Complete Book of Starter Spanish • Grades PreK-1 349

Page 354

Months of the Year Name

Months of the Year

For pages 354-357, use the word bank to write the Spanish month on the line below each English month. Then, in the box, draw a picture of something that happens in that month of the year.

Word Bank

agosto	septiembre	noviembre	mayo
junio	enero	octubre	febrero
marzo	julio	diciembre	abril

January enero	**Pictures will vary.**
February febrero	
March marzo	

354 Complete Book of Starter Spanish • Grades PreK-1

Page 355

Months of the Year   Name

Months of the Year

April **abril**	**Pictures will vary.**
May **mayo**	
June **junio**	

Complete Book of Starter Spanish • Grades PreK-1   355

Page 356

Months of the Year   Name

Months of the Year

July **julio**	**Pictures will vary.**
August **agosto**	
September **septiembre**	

356   Complete Book of Starter Spanish • Grades PreK-1

Page 357

Months of the Year   Name

Months of the Year

October **octubre**	**Pictures will vary.**
November **noviembre**	
December **diciembre**	

Complete Book of Starter Spanish • Grades PreK-1   357

Page 359

Seasons   Name

Winter

These are things you wear in **invierno**.

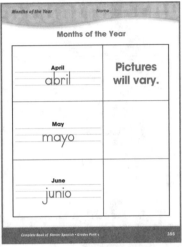

bufanda   abrigo   mitón

Draw something else you wear in **invierno**.

Pictures will vary.

Complete Book of Starter Spanish • Grades PreK-1   359

Page 360

Seasons   Name

Winter

Draw something that you like to do in **invierno**.

Pictures will vary.

360   Complete Book of Starter Spanish • Grades PreK-1

Page 362

Seasons   Name

Spring

These are things you see in **primavera**.

paraguas   lluvia   flor

Draw something else you see in **primavera**.

Pictures will vary.

362   Complete Book of Starter Spanish • Grades PreK-1

Answer Key

Page 363

Page 365

Page 367

Page 373

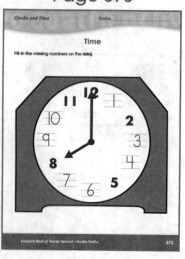

Page 374

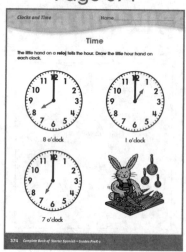

Page 375

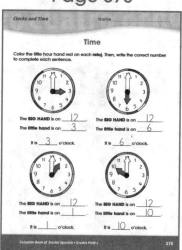